Grandpa ~
Thank you
on my editing team.

Harold

braiding generations

BRAIDING
GENERATIONS

A Grandfather
Breaks the Code

HAROLD BATTENFIELD

Yorkshire Publishing

ISBN: 978-1-942451-10-5 - Book
978-1-942451-11-2 - eBook
Harold Battenfield
Braiding Generations
A Grandfather Breaks the Code

Published in the United States by
Yorkshire Publishing
6271 E. 120th Court, Suite 200
Tulsa, OK 74137
www.yorkshirepublishing.com

Text Design: Lisa Simpson

For Mary

Grandkids occasionally stretched out with me on the roof of our house. We visited in the shade of large oak trees whose branches pumped up and down in the breeze. Whenever talking slowed or stopped, I felt a need to pick up the chatter.

"One time two mean dogs chased me up a tree," I began in one such moment.

"Papa, you've already told us that story," Lauren said.

"Tell you what, kids.
Sometimes I can't remember if I've told you a story or not. Maybe I told a story to just one of you and can't remember which kid I told. From now on if you've heard the story, don't roll your eyes or be too polite to say anything. Just stick up one finger. Like this."

I sat up and pointed to the sky with my right index finger.

"In fact," I continued, "if you've heard the story twice, stick up two fingers. Okay?"

I focused on the largest oak tree by the peak of the roof.

"You know, we could build a good zipline from that tree by the edge of the roof across the yard and end over there on the other side of the yard. What do you think?"

Ten fingers on each grandkid splayed up to the sky.

Table of Contents

⟶

THE EDUCATION OF A GRANDFATHER

A GRANDFATHER BREAKS THE CODE

√ LiBRARY CONTEST

THE EDUCATION
OF A GRANDFATHER

My Daddy's River

On Saturday afternoons the Cisco Kid, Red Ryder, and Lash LaRue fought cattle rustlers and land grabbers in Muskogee's darkened Broadway Theatre. Off-screen little white dots scurried up and down the aisles: kernels of popcorn rustled by theater mice back to their own hole-in-the-wall hideouts. The movies were entertaining, but my daddy's real-life adventures along the Illinois River far surpassed any action trapped in celluloid.

During the early years of statehood, my daddy grew up outside Tahlequah, Oklahoma, near the banks of the Illinois River. Surrounded by beautiful gravel-bottom, spring-fed creeks, the rocky land of what was once known as Indian Territory allowed only subsistence farming. Life was often harsh and lonely in the frontier culture. He attended a one-room school through the eighth grade. Further grades offered in Tahlequah were an impractical, two-day journey in a horse-drawn wagon, but the knowledge he gained from experiences in that river valley could not be taught in a classroom.

After the Cherokees were forced to walk over 2,200 miles on the Trail of Tears from North Carolina to Oklahoma, a tragic chapter in American history, they established their capital in Tahlequah in 1839. My daddy grew up among these Indian children. He fished the river and hunted with his dog. I listened with envy to his enchanting stories of living by the river and wanted a connection across our father-son generation gap. I yearned for a time and place long past that could give me love and comfort.

Ꮖ

Gasoline was cheap when my daddy took our family for country drives on Sunday afternoons. Whether we headed north, south, east or west, we always ended up on the banks of the Illinois River, one hour from our home in Muskogee.

Tired of chewing dust in the backseat, my older sisters and I piled out of the car whenever he parked on the side of the road, following him across a pasture to another of his remembered vantage points. My mother would stay behind to spread a blanket under the shade of a giant sycamore and make bologna sandwiches with white bread, lettuce, onions, and mayonnaise. She had heard his river stories ever since they first dated along these banks.

∾

One Sunday in 1946 when I was nine, we stood on a six-foot bank overlooking the river. The three of us kids stood silent as our daddy's mind drifted back to when he was a kid, right there. After a pause, he began. "I was fourteen years old."

He halted briefly, gazing upriver, as if waiting for a memory to drift into sight. When he spoke, he didn't seem to care if we listened. Yes or no, he would give voice to the memory churning in his mind, the conversation he was having with himself.

"After a good rain lastin' several days, sometimes the river rose right outta its banks. Not a big flood, but enough to float off boats that'd been pulled up on the banks 'stead of tied. Because it weren't a long river, high water went down overnight."

He looked back at us. "Right here on this curve was the best place to watch for flat-bottomed boats floatin' away followin' high water. Now I'm not talkin' 'bout store-bought boats like you see in movies that used tar to plug them cracks. We didn't have no tar for the leaks. Ours all leaked, just a matter how much." He held his hand up in front of his face to show us the cracks between his fingers. "Just like 'em cracks 'tween my fingers. Somebody's bailin' all the time. All boats was homemade from local timber, so no two boats just alike. As far back as I can remember, I only seen one painted and it was faded red. Must have been left over from a schoolhouse."

He took a few steps closer to the edge and looked upriver to confirm his location. "Yep, this was the best waitin' spot to get a boat floatin' downriver. It was finders-keepers in those days. Boats didn't have no names or registration numbers. Nothin' was locked, includin' houses and cars. We weren't greedy. If a better boat come along, we let the first one go for someone else down the river. This weren't stealin'."

While he talked I wondered why I didn't look like him. His hair was combed the only way I had ever seen it, straight back. He didn't need a mirror; he could comb his hair in the dark. I wore a burr cut with too many cow-licks to comb. Most of all, I wanted a full masculine neck like his, instead of my pencil neck. I wanted to look like my daddy.

"The only gun our family had was a double-barrel 12-gauge shotgun that was held onto the stock in two places with bailin' wire." He looked around to confirm we had not gone back to the car. Sometimes he paused, not as though he had forgotten details, but as though he were watching himself as a kid. We stood in silence. By now he held that imaginary shotgun in his hand and was sighting down the barrel. "A double-barrel shotgun has two triggers, one for each barrel. You pulled the first trigger. Bam!" He jumped from the imaginary kick of the barrel. We jumped away from his gun.

"Then you moved your finger to the second trigger. The problem with this gun was a hair trigger. When the first shell was fired, it jarred off the second shell. Bam! Bam! The first kick would throw me off balance and the second would knock me down. I got 'round this by leanin' into the first shot just as I pulled the trigger."

He pointed to the water below. "About ten ducks wuz on the water, right there. I crawled in the weeds up to the edge of this bank right where we're standin'. With both barrels loaded I jumped up and leaned into the first shot as I pulled the trigger. The damn thang misfired and I fell off this bank into that river, right here. Them ducks got away and I broke one of the wires holdin' the gun stock."

My daddy told the story like it happened yesterday and we needed to know the details. He had told us this tale so many times we could only offer courtesy grins. He shared these stories because they were important to him. My sisters heard charming yarns, but I heard magic and lingered on the riverbank.

∽

Ten years after Mary and I married, my mother, who understood my lifelong love of the Illinois River, discovered an old hardback book at a garage sale. She purchased *Where the Red Fern Grows* for fifteen cents, signed the inside back cover, and gave it to me. The book jacket said Wilson Rawls's story was loosely based on his own life that unfolded along the Illinois River near Tahlequah, the same river-bottom lands where my daddy grew up. I wanted to believe his character, Billy Coleman, and my daddy knew each other.

Here was an opportunity to expose my girls to their roots. I fantasized about reading the book with them, telling them about standing on the riverbank and hearing my daddy's hair-trigger shotgun story. Then they would understand my background and ask me to take them floating down my special river. I had more than enough reason to read the book to my daughters.

Mary was a third-grade teacher. I told her I wanted to spend more quality time with our daughters by reading to them. Was *Where the Red Fern Grows* an appropriate book? I hadn't yet read it myself. Actually, I wanted Mary to be proud of me. She thought for a moment, then rolled her eyes, implying it was about time. "You pick it, you read it," she said. "Just as long as you're reading to them is what's important."

∽

Lori and I snuggled on one end of the couch. She was in the third grade, old enough to read, old enough to be a good listener. "This was my daddy's river. This is also my river," I said, opening the book.

As far as I knew, this was just a simple kid's book set along the Illinois River. I quickly realized the plot was intense as it followed the adventures of a twelve-year-old boy and his dogs. Billy Coleman had worked and saved for two years to buy his two blue-tick hound puppies: a brother and sister, Old Dan and Little Ann. The three of them hunted together, explored the shoreline, and shared adventures in the rocky river-bottom. Their bond grew strong. Big Dan was bold and reckless, Little Ann smart and loving. Big Dan would not eat until Little Ann also had food. Throughout the book, Lori and I rooted for Billy in his adventures and fell in love with the dogs.

Five pages from the end, my voice began to quiver. Tears stalked our eyes. Lori and I began crying together. I gulped for air trying to turn a page. Dual sobs overrode words. I could not see the pages. In the kitchen, Mary realized the rhythm of our sounds had changed. "What's the problem?" she called. "I'll be right there." Entering the living room, she gave us a puzzled look.

Lori pushed herself up from a slumped position. With shoulders shaking, she sobbed as she explained that Big Dan had a fight with a mountain lion. He jumped right in front of Little Ann and Billy and saved their lives but Big Dan was seriously wounded and died the next day. Billy buried him behind the barn. Little Ann lay down on Big Dan's grave and refused to eat or move. Two days later she died of a broken heart and Billy buried her next to Big Dan.

I was supposed to be the strong father in charge, but I looked at Mary and, sobbing, handed over the book. "Would you read?" I asked her, managing only a nod. Mary sat between us, entered the story cold, and read the last five pages aloud.

Billy's family had already made plans to move before the dogs died. Before they left, Billy visited the graves behind the barn for the last time. To his surprise a small red fern was growing between his dogs. According to an old Indian legend, these ferns are extremely rare and grow only where there is exceptional love.

Six years later Amy began third grade. I exercised my fatherly duty by reading *Where the Red Fern Grows* to her. Knowing the ending I expected to make it through the last five pages this time. With seven pages left, I grew apprehensive but figured I could gut it out. Two pages later the contest was on for who was crying the most, Amy or me. I couldn't cry and read at the same time. Between sobs, I managed a quivered yell, "Mary?"

❧

Another generation passed. Lori married and bore sons. When the twins started third grade, I was ready. With credentials of more maturity, life experiences, and graying hair, I imagined myself as a strong grandfather role model for Max and Sam. By the time I reached the last five pages, Max and Sam were punching pillows. They sounded like wailers at a Middle-Eastern funeral. Max retreated under the covers while Sam hurled himself off his bed onto the floor, still hugging a pillow. "Lori," I yelled with a shaky voice.

Lori stumbled on the first page she tried to read. Her voice quivered as she called to her husband. "Doug? Come help us." Unfamiliar with the story, he read the final pages undisturbed.

Three years later, I read the book to Lori's youngest son, Jack. By then I didn't even try to finish the book and asked Max to stand by for the final five pages. He handled the first page okay but stumbled during the final four.

Next in line came Amy's Lauren. This reading unfolded like Jack's, except Amy stood by to read the ending with tears in her eyes and a weak voice.

I read to Amy's Keegan and Grant, the youngest grandkids, when each entered third grade. By this time tradition demanded I read two chapters of the book at their house on Wednesday nights while they lay in bed, with Amy prepared to read the final four pages. The reading had become a rite of passage, accepting the consequence of crying together. We cried for the grief and loss experienced by characters we had grown to love.

When Grant and I finished reading the book, his head was still on my arm as he began sliding over that slippery bank into slumber. He made a one-legged kick to stay awake.

"Papa? When you die, can I have the book to read to my children and grandkids?"

"I would like that." And then I cried.

∽

Kids plus dogs make good stories. Reading a simple book about a kid and his dogs to my children and grandkids, however, was never simple. My two daughters signed the book under my mother's inscription, adding the year the book was read to them. My grandkids also signed and dated the book, in chronological order and third-grade script. If a fire ever occurs in our house, what will I save first? The family photo album and *Where the Red Fern Grows.*

Running clear from the foothills of the Ozark Mountains southwest into Oklahoma, the Illinois River became my river, connecting my daddy to my grandkids. On its banks, generations of our family have continued to camp, fish and tell tall tales. Those campfire stories and memories tie me to this place. When I sit on the bank of the Illinois, I hear the voice that called my daddy. When I stand in its shallow rapids, I feel the river twisting over and around my ankles. Over and around again it twists, braiding generations of my family together drop by drop.

Grant, Harold, Keegan, Lauren

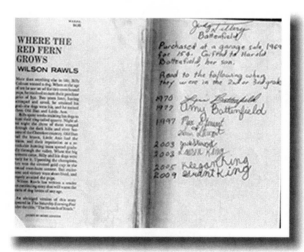

Sharing *Where The Red Fern Grows*
Through the Years

In Tall Cotton

Mary and I sat drinking coffee in Mom's kitchen. "Son," she said, "I have somethin' to tell you that's been in my craw a long time." We prepared ourselves for bad news.

"Decades ago your daddy and I talked about tellin' you and your sisters about our Dust Bowl years in California but never got around to it. You were too young to remember and we were too embarrassed to bring it up. The longer we waited, the harder it got. And here it is 1988 already. Your daddy passed eight years ago, so now the tellin' falls on me."

"It's okay, Mom. Tell us whatever it is you want us to know."

Born in February 1937 during the cotton-picking season in California's San Joaquin Valley, I was carried a week later in a basket from our tent out to the picking fields to join my mother, Julia, and older sisters, Betty and Sue. Company supervisors for the growers used men like my daddy to load heavy bushels of produce onto trucks.

Too young to be effective pickers, six-year-old Betty delivered pails of water to us from a pickup truck on the corner of the field while four-year-old Sue watched over me, shading me from the sun. Mom waddled and stooped as she hoed or picked a row measuring up to a thousand feet long. Betty and Sue moved me along to match her timing so Mom, dehydrated after an hour or more of back-breaking work, could nurse me for a few minutes and rest her back.

Women who gave birth in migrant camps frequently developed urinary tract infections caused by irritation during delivery and chronic dehydration when they returned to the fields. I didn't learn until later that women needed to drink water for bladder infections. Mom described the pain as passing a double-edged razor blade. Yet she drank only after my sisters had their fill. Antibiotics were not available to migrant workers in 1937.

✎

With a shaky voice and moist eyes, Mom began her story.

"Followin' harvest seasons, we moved from camp to camp, picking fourteen hours a day, seven days a week, receiving pennies per pound at the end of each day. On the first of each month, counties gave food commodities to folks like us who couldn't live on the wages paid for workin' in the fields. If we could find a ride to the county warehouse, the government gave us blocks of butter and cheese and large jars of peanut butter."

She chuckled as she leaned forward to run her fingers through my hair and down my neck. "Always wondered if that high fat content isn't what killed your daddy with an early heart attack. I'm surprised you kids have good bones and your teeth didn't fall out."

Mom looked into her coffee cup. "We survived on what the county gave us and our earnings in the field, but near the end of each month, we worried about runnin' out of food too soon. We were some of the luckier ones in the valley, though, not fallin' ill with tuberculosis, pneumonia, or dysentery like so many other families did."

She looked out the window as though the rest of her story waited out there. "There's somethin' else I never told you."

My heart began racing as I imagined unspeakable family secrets. I screwed up my courage. "Whatever it was, it happened a long time ago. Tell us."

"Ever since that time, whenever I watch news of natural disasters like floods, earthquakes and mudslides, and bags of food are thrown from the back of a truck to the hungry, I feel myself crowded in the middle of those people with my hands up. I've never been able to bear the thought that my children might ever have to go through what your daddy and I did."

Her embarrassment stabbed through me. "Because you never spoke of your experience, we kids assumed the subject was off-limits, so we never brought it up. Did you ever tell Daddy about your feelings?"

Mom hesitated. "No. Didn't ever want to go there, but I'm ready now. Time for you to know your history. That's all it is now, history."

Mom went on to tell us the state of California offered a one-way train ticket for pickers and their families from the Dust Bowl to return to their home states. An overabundance of migrant workers, in areas where growers advertised for more hands than needed, had overwhelmed schools, housing, and sanitation. Most migrants didn't have cars; word about the free train fare spread quickly. Even with a free ride for the entire family, many couldn't afford to buy enough food for several days to take with them, let alone buy train food. Since pickers were paid at the end of each day, the most money anyone ever had at one time was at the end of one day.

Mom paused, dragged her index finger around the cup rim, turned away and gazed out the window again. After taking a sip of coffee, she turned back to face us.

"We weren't planning to leave California until one morning when we woke up to find your hungry sisters ate all the cheese and peanut butter during the night. Without any bread to put the remaining dairy butter on, we passed around a spoon, taking turns dipping and eating the rest of the butter. That was the mornin' your daddy and I decided to catch the train to Oklahoma the followin' week. It would be the end of the month and we could get our com- modities from the county and have enough to eat on the train. At the last minute, when no one was watching, we pocketed a few ripe peaches from the back of a truck. I remember laughin' and your daddy sayin' we didn't have anything to sell and nothing to leave behind except sad stories. Everythin' we had in the world we wore on our backs or swept off the floor and stuffed into a paper sack."

"When was this?" Mary asked.

"June of '41. Harold was four. Pearl Harbor was attacked six months after we returned."

Mary and I waited patiently to hear more about my heritage and the family she had married into. I was beginning to understand how much a product I am of parents who lived through the Great Depression and Dust Bowl.

"We settled back in Oklahoma," Mom explained. "We just didn't have anywhere else to go. Your granddad, Oscar, offered us a two-room house and forty acres to farm as sharecroppers. He also left behind two old but workable plow horses and a plow. The horses knew how to pull together. That was important."

ᏔᎭᎤ

My parents had left dust-stricken Oklahoma for the green valleys of California with dreams of returning home with money in their pockets. Instead of money, they returned with one more mouth to feed. Our family of five settled among relatives in a rural farming community six miles north of Wagoner, Oklahoma, as much for moral support as for physical support.

Others who had taken the same journey used the words "California," "sweat," "hunger," and "dread" interchangeably, all with negative connotations. "California" in particular was used in comparisons. For instance, if someone wouldn't shut up, I often heard, "I'd hate to drive all the way from here to California with her!"

Like soldiers coming home from battle, returning migrant workers did not want to relive the experience by talking about it. Their trauma was not easily shared with family descendants, only referred to in short, soft tones with other survivors. Unlike soldiers, however, migrants battled with their families alongside them in the fields, families of hungry children scrabbling in the dirt.

I am not sure if I remember or simply think I remember the long train ride back to Oklahoma on the AT&SF. What I remember for sure was my first neon sign in Wagoner: a bright and shiny curved arrow. I thought I'd died and gone to heaven. At least a more exciting life.

Our new homestead consisted of a living room and kitchen, two-hundred square feet in all. The kitchen had a cast iron wood stove and a table. Outside was a well with water unfit for drinking, an outhouse, and a three-sided shed that housed the two horses. Mom's mother, Rosie, loaned us a milk cow, so we needed room for three animals. Although the old cow was smaller, she bullied one of Oscar's horses out during bad weather. Chickens and a pig wandering the yard rounded out our basic survival needs.

My sisters and I attended a one-room schoolhouse down the road. The teacher lived in Wagoner and came over every day to teach twelve students in grades one through eight. Her daughter and I became best friends in first grade. No children attended grades two or three. Sue was in the fourth grade and Betty in the sixth. My first exposure to education was with a best friend and siblings by my side, my siblings encouraged by the teacher to tell me to do my work. We all heard the same lessons year after year with increasing comprehension. Together we ate lunch by the stove in the back of the room and drank water from the well outside.

For years I thought rooms should be decorated with rags sticking out from the walls. Mom stuffed old rags into any wall crack to keep out either cold or dust, depending on the season. The largest gaps were where the wall planks joined the ceiling. For these high spaces, she stood on her toes on a chair and stuffed rags into holes using a kitchen fork. She would never forget the penetrating dust that found its way through any crack, regardless of size. She often set the table with plates upside down to be turned over at the last minute before serving.

Our living room functioned like a motel room; we lived in the room where we slept. Mom and Daddy slept in the only real bed, and my sisters and I made do with second-hand folding military cots. Usually I slept on a cot with Sue, but sometimes I squeezed between my parents to keep warm.

Daddy snored so loudly that if he went to sleep first, the rest of us were doomed. Betty would slip off her cot, shake him enough to partially wake him and stop the snoring, then race back to bed in an attempt to beat him to sleep. I propped my head on an elbow and watched him snore. When he exhaled, his lips looked like boiling oatmeal.

In summer we rolled off the cots to the coolest place in the house—the floor—and slept in pools of our own sweat. Sometimes we pulled the cots outside onto the grass for Mom and Daddy while we three kids slept atop blankets on the porch. The adults awarded themselves the cots because breezes could move above and below them, plus mosquitoes could not bite through the canvas. We kids traded cooler air for mosquitoes, and I lay in the dark envying our cow and horses with their swishing tails. I learned to wrap a thin towel around my face and breathe through my open fist over my mouth. Mosquitoes would not crawl into a hole, or so I hoped.

Down the road apiece another two-room abandoned house like ours rested on the corner of a pasture. That winter Daddy decided to add it to our house. Using the plow horses, he dragged the house over six rolling fence posts. When he pulled forward enough to expose the back log, he rotated that one to the front and pulled forward again. The slow drag across the pasture required two days for the addition to reach the back of our house.

With a borrowed handsaw, he made a cut through both houses at the same time. In theory the doors should have been perfectly aligned, but opposing wall openings were offset by two inches. Alignment for plumbing and electricity was not an issue as utilities were not yet available. Overnight the size of our house doubled. We had both a front door and a back door.

Overflowing with memories, I grinned across the table at Mom. "I remember the day you and I stood outside admiring our newly-remodeled four-room house."

"So do I. You were too small to help your daddy pull the house but you could take him Kerr jars filled with cool well water from the schoolhouse spring. He could drink a whole quart in one sittin'."

"After watching him move a house and drink that much water, I figured my daddy could do anything," I said.

"Anythin' he set his mind to," she said. "That was forty-seven years ago. I remember standin' with arms across my chest, proud of our new home, wipin' tears with my apron, and tellin' you we were in tall cotton now."

Sue, Harold, Betty

Crawdads & Crows

In February 1944 my grandfather, Oscar Battenfield, asked me a simple question on my seventh birthday. He and my grandmother lived on a small farm thirty minutes outside of town where we now lived. "Harold, why don't you spend some time on the farm with me and your grandma Eller come summertime?"

"Yeah, Grandpa!"

I imagined riding the family horse, milking the cows, and driving the tractor from my grandpa's lap. Hollywood couldn't have written a better script for a boy on his first trip away from home.

After my parents dropped me off for the week, I stood silent. Oscar had not the foggiest idea how to greet me. We stared at one another. "Hi, Harold," he said.

I tilted my head toward Eller in her scratchy faded sack-cloth dress. She moved to my side and, keeping her distance, laid an arm across my shoulder and stared down without expression. "Glad you could come."

Oscar patted my head.

"Have a look around the place while I make lunch," Eller said. Both grandparents walked away and left me standing.

A tractor slumped in the weeds between the house and barn, its steering wheel long gone. Two cars without wheels sat nearby, their disintegrating seats exposing sharp, rusty springs. Across the road was an old muddy creek! I couldn't leave it alone and promptly slipped off the bank and ended waist-high in mud and water. I trudged around before finding a good place to climb out.

Back at the house, Eller took one look at me and said, "Boy, you been playin' with the hog? How you get so dirty so fast? Wherever you been, don't go back." She wiped my mouth with her apron and raised her voice. "Oscar, draw up some water for a bath." To me she said, "Let's have them clothes. I'm gonna wash 'em while your bath water warms."

The clothes on my back were scheduled to be worn for three days, but I had scuttled the plans before lunch on day one. Eller drew water into a bucket, stripped off my clothes and washed them with homemade lye soap. She rinsed and fed them through a hand-cranked wringer nailed to a tree stump. Snapping her wrists, she popped my clothes up and down to drive out wet creases and hung them on a line to dry in the sun.

Soon the washtub water was warm. Next to the clothesline, I washed in a tub of soft well water using store-bought soap. Eller told me lye soap would burn my skin. Without benefit of a towel, I sat naked on the rock step outside the front door with my knees drawn to my chin and arms about my ankles, waiting another half hour for my clothes to dry. Now I smelled like my grandparents, neither good nor bad, just family.

In the middle of the first night I had to pee. Between me and the outhouse were weeds and black silence and who knew what else. My heart raced. The glow from a half moon was not nearly bright enough to lighten my fears. I didn't make it across the yard. Now I had a new fear: getting in trouble for peeing in the yard.

No sooner did I fall back asleep when someone shook my leg. "Time to get up, Harold. Eller has our breakfast ready."

Eller had fried a half pound of bacon and saved the grease to fry a dozen eggs. With an easy flip, she stacked the eggs high on a plate like pancakes.

Oscar poured his coffee into the saucer and blew across the steaming liquid, then drank directly from the saucer without spilling a drop. We had all the eggs, biscuits smeared with blackberry jelly, and bacon we could eat. While they unknowingly entertained me, I ate using my right hand and kept my left busy scratching chigger bites from my night trip in the grass.

Oscar scooted his chair from the table just as I finished eating. "Come on, Harold, we're goin' to the barn."

I traced his steps as he fed the hog, cow, horse, and chickens. The animals came to us because we had the feed. The most Oscar had to say all morning was when he called the hog. "Soooie!" The hog followed our every step like a friendly, fat puppy. I enjoyed the animals because they were company. The hog grunted while the chickens pecked and squawked together. I wondered if this was all we were going to do. After feeding time, Oscar was done with me just like he was done with feeding the animals.

∽

More than homesick, I was disappointed and lonely. I was used to my neighborhood buddies keeping me busy from morning until bedtime. We ran in a leaderless herd from one yard to the next playing made-up games.

On the farm I wanted to ride on Oscar's shoulders while holding onto his forehead and be high enough to see over the top rail of the fence into the barnyard, to look over the weeds as far as the eye could see, to walk with him and have him ruffle my hair as I tried to milk the cow, to ride that old horse and have him brag on me. I wanted him to give me a chore, however simple. By the second day I assumed every day would be the same. My dream of fun at the farm began to fade.

∽

The next afternoon Oscar turned a scary-looking knife back and forth in his hand. "Know what this is?" I shrugged my shoulders. "A razor. Nobody uses a straight razor any more. Don't touch it. Too sharp for you." I stepped back.

Oscar poured Eller's leftover cooking water into a pan and went out the back door. He sat the pan on a tub turned upside down, pulled a small mirror from his pocket and hung it on a nail on the corner of the house. He sharpened his straight razor by dragging it down a black strap, flipping it over and pulling it up the strap with the grace of a musician's bow on a violin. The slap-drag, slap-drag created an

31

unfamiliar rhythm and sound. Oscar gripped the black handle, and the edge of the razor seemed to glisten more with each slap-drag. I kept my distance. In my pocket was a sharp pocketknife for whittling, but his razor was more than a knife. Almost evil.

The house had no porch, only a flat sandstone rock as a single step to the front door. After supper the second night, I hoped to sit on it and listen to my grandparents talk about their childhoods like my parents did. But Eller stayed inside washing dishes while he pulled a kitchen chair outside, leaned against the house and swatted flies, targeting anything within reach. He never counted his victims, never made a game of it, such as a two-for-one swat, and never commented about the flies. Not looking at me, he waited with cocked wrist for a fly to land. "Don't you go climbin' around in that old barn because it's full of rusty nail," he said. I nodded. "Don't have a saddle for the horse and can't ride bareback because the bridle is broken. Besides, she's too old." I nodded. "Look out for them water moccasins 'round the stock pond. I seen a big rattlesnake by the creek." I nodded and headed straight for the creek.

Evening light gave me the opportunity to walk up and down its banks, exploring the muddy still waters with a stick and making plans.

The next morning, armed with a bucket, piece of string, and a slice of tough bacon from Eller, I discovered my own fishing hole. Weighed down with a small rock and dropped in the water, bacon enticed a crawdad. The place was alive with crawdads to be teased up with their hungry pinchers hanging onto the bacon. Big ones and little ones filled the bottom of my bucket. Once the crawdad rate of return began to slip, I sat on the bank digging mud off my shoes with a stick. My gut felt empty. I was homesick. Down the creek crows foraged under a pecan tree. If I could catch crawdads on a string, why not catch a crow? If I could get a crow to swallow corn attached to the string, I figured I just might be able to catch one like a fish.

I carefully tied a kernel of corn on the crawdad string and placed the bait under the pecan tree. Eller hollered that lunch was ready. After running to the house to gulp down my food, I hurried back to check out the crow that would be on my line. A crow had picked the kernel out of the string loop. I tried to tie a tighter loop, but it continued to slip off. Borrowing a large needle from Eller, I threaded it with string which passed easily through the kernel. Eller filled my small hand with more corn to bait the area.

Of course the crows took flight when I approached, but they would return, especially after I scattered corn in their feeding area. My bait was in the middle with its free end of string tied to a large limb lying on the ground. Crows refused to land while I was anywhere nearby, so I hid behind another tree. At last one crow approached cautiously, hovering before settling down at the edge of the corn. He hopped and pecked at a kernel. The cawing began, one crow answering another until a whole flock flew in to join their scout. My heart raced. They pecked and hopped around picking up corn. I was afraid to blink.

Finally one picked up the bait but flicked it away as he took flight. The bully of the flock grabbed it in mid-air. He must have swallowed the kernel because he suddenly did a flip before recovering and flying off. The flock took wing squawking, "Danger! Danger!" I ran to check my line and found it had broken close to the knot. Somewhere a big crow was flying around with string hanging out the side of his mouth. Although the crows did not return the rest of the week, I had salvaged my day.

∾

After catching crawdads and almost catching crows, I was a curious seven-year-old boy who resorted to spending long hours examining fence posts inside the chicken yard. Strands of barbed wire laced the top of the posts together, and chicken wire enclosed the bottom half of the fence. Eller walked across the yard in a crouched position, spreading her arms to corner a chicken. The chosen bird must have recognized Eller had come not to feed but to be fed because the bird began running, squawking, and flapping its wings. Eller grabbed its legs just above the ankles, trapping them with one hand between her right thumb and index finger and the other between her ring and little fingers. The chicken was doomed. The fear-stricken flock began running and squawking. I ran away with them to hide behind bushes within the fenced yard.

Holding the chicken by its head, Eller swung her hand in a quick small arc with a snap of the wrist at the bottom of the arc. She pitched the chicken's head near the fence and wiped the blood from her hands on her apron. She saw me peering around the bush.

"Don't worry, the other chickens will eat that head," she said.

The headless chicken jumped and flopped its wings while blood spurted out of what remained of its neck. I had seen my daddy shoot a squirrel and fish flopping on a hook, but nothing like this. Although the bush remained between me and the flopping chicken, I backed away. Pressed against a fence post, I vomited.

After the beheading, Eller heated a pot of water back in the kitchen. She plucked large feathers from the chicken's wings and tail. When the water came to a boil, she dropped the bird into the pot. Heat loosened the soft small feathers for easy plucking, but the awful smell of the wet, scorched feathers ranked right up there with the gore of the headless flopping chicken. Without wasting anything, she fed the intestines to the hog and cooked the neck, gizzard, heart, and other parts I didn't recognize. That night we had volume: chicken, milk, and cornbread, but not what I wanted most—conversation. Once again at the table, I searched their faces for a clue, trying to decide if they were mad at each other or me. This meal was as solemn and silent as the others. "Good chicken, Grandma."

Eller came closer to smiling than Oscar.

Each day on the farm passed slower than all the days spent waiting for Christmas.

⚬⚬⚬

My great uncle Eli, Oscar's brother, stopped by one morning for a visit. The men talked in slow syllables without inflection, each sounding more like an echo of the other rather than a separate person. They squatted in the shade of the house with a right buttocks resting on the heel of the right shoe. Oscar pulled a pouch of Bull Durham tobacco and cigarette paper from the pocket of his Roundhouse bib overalls and rolled his own. He dragged his tongue across the paper to create a seal and crimped and licked both ends to prevent tobacco from falling out. Holding the new cigarette in his right hand, he closed the tobacco pouch by pulling on the purse string with his teeth as easily as tying his shoe while staying in the conversation. They allowed me to eavesdrop on their conversation of poor government and bad weather. Personal stories of survival through the Dust Bowl days twined around stories of the Great Depression. The hard times were not stories told but stories relived.

They never acknowledged my presence and talked with their heads down, looking at the still dust, pausing for what felt like days after every story. Occasionally the listener nodded his head. How could the men sit and say nothing? I couldn't tolerate silence, couldn't sit on my foot, and couldn't smoke, so I lost interest and wandered off for more action.

◊

Oscar and Eller kept a single kerosene lamp in their bedroom, the only light at night. They used the lamp like a flashlight when light was needed, but not for play. Kerosene cost money so we went to bed before dark. My bed was the living room couch with sackcloth sheets and a shotgun hole between my legs. Years before, Oscar had picked up his shotgun by the trigger and blasted the hole now stuffed with feed store rags. My grandparents viewed learning to read and write as the responsibility of schools and kept no books. They did, however, keep a Sears & Roebuck catalogue in the outhouse.

Eller explained the system to me soon after my arrival. "A catalogue can last a family of three a little over three months if no one cheats. Oscar favors the woods for his business, except in bad weather. He considers outhouse walls too confining. How your daily page is folded, torn, or divided is up to you."

Catalogue pages were slick and shiny. I rubbed each one back and forth between my hands or resorted to balling and smoothing it repeatedly to make it softer. On my arrival, the first nineteen pages were already gone. Browsing through the catalogue on the jagged-edged seat that must have been cut out with a hatchet, I discovered bright red Radio Flyer wagons on page thirty-eight and handsome hunting knives on seventy-six.

Two days later the red Radio Flyer wagon page was gone. As the week drew to a close, the shrinking catalog measured my days. On the day of my departure, the hunting knives had been torn out. My parents expected to visit with Oscar and Eller. I wanted to rush directly to our car. Instead I listened politely as my grandparents told my parents how much fun we had and how they looked forward to my return the next summer.

Forcing myself to keep from running to the car with my pillowcase of clothes, I walked over and tossed it into the backseat. I leaned casually against the fender, hoping to send a message to my parents. The four adults strolled toward me in slow motion. Oscar patted me on my head while Eller stood at my side, one arm across my shoulder, always side by side, never closer. I slipped from under her arm and scrambled into the back seat. The adults continued to visit.

Finally we all waved goodbye. As soon as we crested the first hill, I leaned forward to look out the windshield. Somewhere ahead my friends played without me. I looked forward to playing with them again, sleeping without a hole between my legs, and using a toilet seat that didn't pinch.

∽

The following summer Oscar came to visit us. "Harold, when are you going to come spend some time with me and Eller?"

I looked at the ground. "I don't know."

Our family returned to the farm many times for holidays and special occasions, but my parents never mentioned sending me for another lengthy stay. They knew. Neither my grandparents nor I recognized we functioned according to an unwritten code: grandparents were boring. I understood then that grandparents must be more interesting than their competition—the kids' friends. Two generations later I applied the code.

〜

Thirty years later, I smelled Eller in a flea market and tracked the soothing scent to a booth. Sitting in my car with a chunk of newly-purchased lye soap cupped in my hands, I was transported back to the farm, to a day of sitting naked in the sun and smelling Eller's soap as she washed my clothes, to a past I couldn't fully appreciate when I was seven. I scraped soap under my fingernails so I could carry the scent with me the rest of the day, to catch a sniff whenever the chance arose. It smelled like family.

〜

When my twin grandsons, Max and Sam, turned seven, I took them to the old farm to show them a part of their heritage. Nothing remained of the homestead except a depression where the storm cellar had been and foundation rocks along the outline of the house which must have burned as it was too rickety to have been moved. The barn was reduced to a pile of more rotten lumber with rusty, crumbly nails. The decayed wringer was still nailed to a stump. Only one pecan tree was left standing, but the old muddy creek showed nature's staying power.

"There's the creek I told you about with all the crawdads, and over past the creek is that tree where I tried to catch a crow."

The twins ran up and down the banks, probing the water for crawdads with sticks. "Papa, where can we get some string and bait to fish for crawdads?"

"Hmm. I just happen to have some string and strips of bacon in the car."

As the three of us chattered and fished, my eyes roamed over the remains of what was once here. I saw Oscar in the barn feeding the animals, Eller in the house plucking chicken feathers, and me, well, I was standing right here by the old muddy creek, playing all by myself. This time was different. This time I had playmates.

"Got one, Papa! Now what do we do with him?"

I had broken the old code.

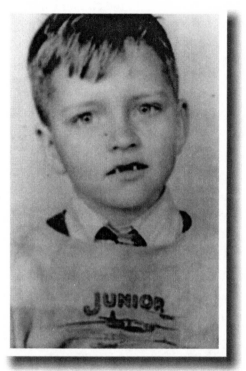

Harold in First Grade

Sleeping Arrangements

Mom was in her mid-sixties when Daddy died of a heart attack in 1980. A year later I realized that if I were going to chronicle our family history, I had better do it soon. With a new video camera in hand, I stood with Mom in front of our first house in Muskogee while the camera hummed.

"Our house never had a bed empty long enough to lose its warmth," she said, pressing her fingers over her lips to stifle a giggle. "Ten people lived here at once. We had three bedrooms and one bath and we managed."

Her eyes sparkled as she brushed aside her wavy red hair. "This was our first house in Muskogee after your daddy landed a job as a truck driver and you," she said, turning toward the camera, "were in second grade. We bought it with the bank's help. The war was still going on."

⁓

Mom's parents, Rosie and Lowery, were destitute when they moved into one of our three bedrooms. Mom rented another to the wife and three-year-old son of an Army soldier stationed at nearby Camp Gruber until the husband was transferred overseas four months later. Less than a month after they moved out, Mom's niece lost her job in Colorado, so she and her two children moved in with us. We kids slept on a pallet of blankets to soften the living room floor until the family next door loaned us a mattress. I never saw my home as overcrowded. In fact, I was elated to have kids my age with whom to play. During the one year we lived there, Grandpa Lowery died, and the Army family and our cousins moved on. Only Grandma Rosie found a permanent home with us.

Mom and Daddy revisited the frontier philosophy they had developed during the Great Depression and Dust Bowl: a family could survive the worst of times by owning a cow, a pig, and chickens, and by planting a garden, so we moved. The second house provided three bedrooms and one bath on two acres outside of town and the emotional security of a garden and farm animals.

In this house Betty and Sue shared a bedroom, Grandma Rosie had one to herself, and I slept on a collapsible military cot in my parents' room through the sixth grade. Some nights they whispered and giggled. I knew instinctively that whatever was taking place was none of my business.

Four years later my parents understood the dynamics of a changing world. Straddling the two cultures of farming and working in town was impractical. Either our family needed to live in town closer to work, as two salaries were needed to pay the bank loan, or move farther out of town on a real farm.

We moved back to town into yet another house with three bedrooms and one bath. Betty and Sue claimed a bedroom. My parents claimed a room too small to also accommodate me. Therefore, by default, as I entered the seventh grade, I slept in bed with Grandma Rosie in her room. By now she was sixty-five, stooped to less than five feet tall, and weighed 105 pounds. Her quiet demeanor matched her size. To my knowledge she never laughed or cried. I remember only her pleasant, comforting voice. She read the Bible daily by dragging her right index finger below each letter, spelling the word and pronouncing it in a whisper. I never had the nerve to ask her how far she went through school.

A washhouse lit by a single window and screen door stood not twenty feet beyond the house. Moving a narrow bed inside, I spent sweet warm nights sleeping and dreaming alone for three or more months of the year, savoring privacy for the first time in my life. When the nights grew too cold, even with extra blankets, I moved back inside to sleep.

Betty married and left home at age eighteen. One might have expected Sue to share a bed with Rosie, but each wanted to stay in her own bed. This arrangement left me still sleeping with Rosie, sinking deep into her enveloping feather bed that reminded me of Lowery lying on a quilted pad in his coffin at the Bradley-Hunter Funeral Home. Occasionally, when Rosie didn't feel well, I bunked with Sue. When my buddies found out, they wanted to spend the night with me.

Sue followed Betty's pattern. Again one might have expected an empty bedroom for me, but my parents had two surprises late in life, Judy and Paula, who needed her room. Privacy, a concept I knew so little about, was obviously important for baby-making. Sleeping with Grandma Rosie was intended to be a temporary arrangement, but she became my permanent indoor roommate for the seventh through twelfth grades.

On a cool spring night in 1955, while I was dreaming outside in the washhouse, Rosie died in her sleep. Mom washed the sheets, but months passed before I could sleep alone and comfortably in her bed. Without Rosie's quiet easy breathing, the room felt lifeless, as if a treasured clock had stopped. I realized I didn't want that bed to myself after all; I wanted Grandma Rosie.

Three years after Daddy died, Mom married a six-foot-tall, lanky, childless widower named Ray Tillery, the nicest guy in town. Gentle and caring, he taught Mom's young grandkids to play dominoes and always let them win.

An educational seminar in Little Rock, Arkansas, took me from Tulsa through Muskogee, and I planned to spend the night with them. "Our house is your house," Ray said when he opened the front door.

My thirst for an uninterrupted visit with Mom in my quiet childhood home was insatiable. We visited and gossiped over glasses of lemonade well into the evening hours, catching up on our lives and those of neighbors and relatives. Too soon she and Ray were ready for bed. "Now don't you get too busy and forget your family," she said as she stood up.

Not long after they retired to their bedroom, I lingered in their doorway talking. Mom scooted in the bed toward Ray and patted the empty space next to her for me to sit down. While we continued to visit, Ray stared at the ceiling, probably wondering what in the world this middle-aged man was doing sitting on his bed. Mom reached up, patted me on the dome of my head, and slid her hand down the back of my neck. As I slipped down on top of the covers and shared her pillow, she nudged the top of my head with her arm so she could ease it under my neck. I was home again.

She gave me a hug just like she did when I was a little boy—pure comfort. "I was hoping you would do this, Son. You've been so busy, but tonight I get to spend some time with you." The impossible clock turned back and once again we were mother and child. For a few moments responsibility fell from my shoulders. How wonderful her touch would have felt during the years of raising my own family, coping with disease and loss. I had longed for her simple gestures that said, *It's okay. You've done the best you could.*

What does a forty-five-year-old man lying next to his mother in bed with his stepfather on the far side talk about? Stories new and old, all embellished with happy endings. Ray no doubt wondered what kind of a family he had married into. Mom sniffled. My own tears rolled into my ears. I didn't dare move and break the spell. She ran her hand down the back of my neck.

Mom's sniffles broke into snickers, then breath-stealing bursts of laughter. "This is as good as it gets. How do I tell my friends I went to bed with two men at the same time and loved them both?"

The conversation slowed. Stretching out the moment lying there next to Mom but unwilling to overstay my welcome, I kissed her on the cheek, gave her a hug, and reached beyond her to pat Ray. He lay as stiff as a mummy with hands folded across his chest. "Good night to both of you. It's been a hoot."

Mom's voice quivered. "For me, too."

"Thank you, Ray, for sharing Mom with me." He didn't reply, but perhaps he understood my thanks for our journey back to a simpler time.

Feeling a warm connection between present and past, I headed down the hall and around the corner to my old room, considering where life had taken me since my days with Grandma Rosie. After taking a deep breath, I entered the room to the right side of the bed. Wrong side. Having always slept on the left side, I walked around the foot of the bed, crawled in and pulled the covers beneath my chin, reliving my spontaneous, unexpected, bonus visit.

Slowly my right hand slid across the sheets into forbidden territory. I scooted into the unfamiliar middle and spread my arms and legs wide like a skydiver. Then snow angels. Though the entire bed was mine, my body gradually drifted back to the left side. My side, the side without a table lamp to turn on and off, the side where I had yearned for conversation never spoken and time to read long after dark. In those days wishing for a whole bed for myself was beyond the pale of my thinking.

The warmth of my mother's arm moments earlier spilled into the night. Unwilling to fall asleep too quickly, I kneaded the evening. Soon Grandma Rosie was beside me in bed, her soft shallow breaths whispering in the dark. That's when I realized the connection. All the fun projects played out as an adult with my grandkids were spawned by my sleeping arrangements growing up. Forced isolation next to either Rosie or Sue nurtured my imagination. I had not been bored in the dark, but quite the opposite. I was playful, free to journey at my own pace and stop to explore whatever came my way, fantasizing on my own with my castle-building motor idling. Safe from a timer instructing me to "stop it" and "get in line with everyone else," I rarely experienced self-doubt. No critics stood over me while my imagination ran uncensored. No one told me "that's crazy" or "nobody does that."

My imaginings in the dark evolved from indulgence in casual, disjointed thoughts to well-laid-out concrete plans. I designed and built an imaginary tree-house with three floors and a trap door to keep out the bad guys; envisioned an endless row of dominoes falling over the horizon; learned how to swing on a trapeze; and rafted down a big muddy river like Huckleberry Finn. Dreams and imaginings that took root in my childhood bed blossomed into reality two generations later with my daughters and grandkids. I had polished the art of imagination.

∽

A four-drawer chest still occupied the left corner of the bedroom: two drawers for Rosie, two for me. Beyond my blanket-covered toes the same landscape print hung on the nail I had driven into the wall thirty years earlier. The fact that cows grazing in the pasture had not moved any closer to the haystack and crows still perched on the limb of a tree evoked a satisfying sense of permanence. Hanging the picture for Mom, I had dropped it and broken a small lower right-hand corner of the glass. A windowpane in the room was also cracked in its lower right-hand corner. This was my home, broken corners and all.

And then the visage of my daddy stood at the foot of the bed, a ghost as unbidden as that of Jacob Marley. He was watching me pack for college twenty-five years earlier. "Why do you want to go to college?" he asked. "You'll get by."

"You'll get by" had been his mantra in the face of any obstacle, be it a leaky roof, an undependable car, or a broken door hinge. He was always satisfied with the status quo. Never questioning his words of wisdom, I had taken them as gospel even though they made me feel uncomfortable. Respect for my elders prevailed over questions, reason, and logic. Never having heard the terms "prosper," "succeed," or "thrive," I knew the day he watched me pack that there had to be more to life than getting by.

College led me out of my imagination into the larger world of adulthood, marriage, a fulfilling medical career, daughters, and grandkids. It gave me an education no one expected, especially me, and answered Daddy's question at last: I went to college to fulfill my dreams.

He disappeared when I rolled onto the right side of the bed and switched off the lamp.

A comforting smell permeated the darkened room, not strong enough to qualify as the odor of food or elderly people but simply the scent of my childhood home, alive and bustling with family and relations through the decades of our lives, filled with laughter and goodbyes, and yelling to get into the single bathroom. It was the scent of my imagination's wellspring, the dreams that had sprouted in the dark and thrived in the forced isolation next to Grandma Rosie. I gently patted her side of the bed and fell sound asleep.

Grandma Rosie

Beth's Vital Signs

Our daughter's respiration rate increased to fifty-two breaths per minute. Beth's body would collapse from exhaustion with such shallow, unrelenting, rapid respiration. The normal rate for a child twenty months old is eighteen to twenty breaths per minute.

I'm going about this all wrong. This is not the way to determine a trend. I won't check her respiration for another fifteen minutes.

From the fifth floor of the hospital, I looked west over the heliport to traffic and train bridges over the Arkansas River. No action this morning on the heliport but bumper-to-bumper cars jockeyed across the bridge into town. People trying to get to work on time. A freight train heading our way from West Tulsa blew a long and lonesome whistle. The river carved the northeast corner out of Tulsa; behind me an overcast sunrise tried to crack open the morning.

I gnawed my fingernails and buried trembling hands in my pockets. A muscle twitched below my left eye. My shirt, wet with perspiration, stretched cold across my rigid, poker-back shoulders. I turned from the window, took the few steps to Beth's bedside and stared at her. My heart rocketed around in my chest while my mind reeled with numbers. I waited for a downward trend. There had to be a downward trend. Her temperature registered 104.6 degrees, up two tenths of a degree in the last hour. This was not the right trend.

Beth's case was more than a childhood malady of cough, fever, and diarrhea for a few days. Much more. The typical hundreds of red bumps appeared on her arms, legs, and torso, accompanied by loss of appetite, dehydration and general restlessness. Hours after these symptoms appeared, though, her respiration changed. She couldn't seem to catch her breath. When her breaths grew shallow, and her respiration rate and body temperature increased, Mary called our pediatrician and asked if Beth could be brought to his office.

Dr. Walton was a casual friend, six years ahead of me in practice. My professional field in orthopedics did not cross with his in pediatrics, but we visited at social events and sometimes ate together in the cafeteria. Approachable and knowledgeable, he spoke without being dogmatic and listened more than he talked. We lived on his way home from work, so he stopped by after office hours and advised us to take Beth to the hospital due to her dehydration and rapid breathing. "This should take a couple of days. The hospital is the best place to monitor her." Neither Mary nor I expressed our level of concern.

The attending nurse knocked and entered the room. "I'm going to change out the IV and use a different steroid. Then I'm going to change Beth's sheets and bathe her. Would you folks like to help?" All we could do was nod. Experience taught her the power of engaging family in purpose. She didn't dare ask how we were doing as she measured Beth's temperature and urine output.

Mary and I lifted and turned Beth as the nurse changed the sheets. When the nurse started to bathe Beth with a soapy cloth from a basin, Mary suddenly asked, "Can I do that?"

"Certainly." She handed the washcloth to Mary.

Mary and I requested our families not to visit because we didn't want to be asked the same questions we wanted to ask. When anxious family members gather in a room without defined duties, tension magnifies, a phenomenon I witnessed in my years of orthopedic training and practice.

Two knocks on the door, and Dr. Walton leaned in. "Hi, Harold, Mary. May I come in?" The question was rhetorical. "I've been on the phone with Mayo Clinic. They told me we're doing all that can be done. If Beth were there, they'd be doing the same thing, giving steroids to decrease swelling and pressure on her brain."

A long painful silence hung in the air, as though we were all holding our breath. When he spoke again, he seemed far away, his voice almost inaudible. "Do you have any questions?" He buttoned his coat and shifted Beth's chart from one hand to the other.

Mary shook her head. I looked him in the eye. "No, but we thank you."

"Can I do anything to make you more comfortable? Get you some fresh coffee or take one or both of you to the cafeteria?" He clicked his ballpoint pen again and again. "I encourage you to go home and get some rest."

"Thanks, but we'll stay here."

He walked to the door. "Remember, I'm just a phone call away."

Only earlier that month had our blonde-haired twenty-month-old beauty started calling us Mommy and Daddy. I checked her pulse. Increased to 164 beats per minute, it was far too fast to maintain, even for a small child. If this rate continued, her heart would fatigue.

Mary draped herself on the IV side of Beth's bed and stroked the back of her hand as only a loving mother could do. She kissed the front and back of Beth's free hand. Mary's mouth formed the words, "I love you."

Neither of us slept all night. I ached watching Mary watch Beth and noticed, for the first time ever, bags under my wife's eyes. Her delicate fingers slid along Beth's hand, skin to skin, trying desperately to transfer love, energy, and heart. Mary carried this child for nine months, nursed her, fed and rocked her, a commitment of time and purpose I couldn't match. I donated DNA and played with Beth, but Mary nurtured her. A wet spot on the sheet next to Beth's head showed where Mary cried all night.

I'm the father. I'm supposed to take care of my family. I'm a doctor. I'm supposed to take care of others as well as my family. I can't fix the problem. I'm ashamed. I'm scared.

Two weeks earlier, Beth was exposed to chickenpox, a malady so contagious the virus may infect someone on a different aisle in a supermarket.

◊

Beth always smiled so much during the day I wondered if she smiled in her sleep, so I watched both girls sleep in their cribs to confirm that neither smiled. Beth was still young enough, though, to retain an angelic expression with her deep, rhythmic breaths. Potty training came easier for Beth because she could imitate an older sister. If Lori acted like she was reading, Beth held a book and did the same. Regardless of what Mary served at the table, if Lori ate it, Beth ate it. When Lori gave a two-syllable squeal, Beth was her echo. She loved to be touched and hugged, and gave warm hugs followed by a kiss on my cheek. She expected me to reciprocate.

During the weeks prior to her exposure, she entered into our family's rite of passage: a pillow fight. Understanding the fun, Beth followed Lori, squealing and hurling herself on the couch as I stalked both of them with a snarl and a bed pillow cocked high. I attacked them repeatedly with my pillow. "Take that. And that. And that." Lori rolled off the couch and ran down the hall with Beth on her heels, their melodic little-girl squeals filling the house with delight. Squatting on both knees, I threw two couch pillows striking them from behind without knocking them down. "Okay, I'm going to get serious now—as soon as I get my breath." Before I knew it, they returned to the living room armed with pillows and grins.

Thirty-one years old and in my second year of practice, I was still anxious to prove my value to the world as the junior partner of three orthopedic surgeons in a busy practice. On the other hand Mary was a stream of calm, flowing water with enough depth to absorb the turmoil caused by rocks below.

Mary remained consistent from the first day I watched her skip a stone when she was a sophomore and I a junior at Northeastern State University in the foothills of the Ozarks near the cool, spring-fed, clear, gravel-bottom Illinois River, ideal for floating on tubes and playing. If we boarded a bus of strangers, in short time she knew everyone's name and something about each person, while they knew little about her. She knew more people at social events than I did. I was often referred to as "Mary's husband."

Through seven years of marriage, she supported my work, shielding me from distractions at home. When she smiled, her whole head grinned. I could tell from behind if she was grinning by the tilt of her head. Optimism protected us both from hard knocks. We figured the worst was behind us and expected to board the bullet train through life.

∽

Relieved to be taking Beth to the hospital environment where I thrived, worked, and matured, I could stop by several times a day to check on both Beth and Mary. Based on the combination of history, laboratory tests, consultations, and examinations, Beth was diagnosed with Reyes Syndrome. The viral infection is a rare complication of childhood chickenpox affecting all organs of the body, especially harmful to the brain and liver, with an acute increase in pressure within the brain. Defined as a two-phase illness because warning signs occur in conjunction with a prior viral infection, such as the flu or chickenpox, further symptoms include persistent vomiting, listlessness, irritability, confusion, or loss of consciousness. Cause unknown, no cure was available in 1971. The use of aspirin to treat viral illness increases the risk of developing Reyes Syndrome. When her fever first spiked, I had given Beth a baby aspirin. Successful management includes protecting the brain against irreversible damage by reducing brain swelling. If the patient passes into a coma, the prognosis is grave.

The second night, Dr. Walton was so concerned with Beth that he discussed her case with Dr. Ray Greer, an ear, nose, and throat specialist who examined her. "If she doesn't improve in the next several hours, she will need a tracheotomy. Call me at any hour, including in the middle of the night." Beth was in a coma when Dr. Walton placed the call at 4:30 a.m. Mary and I assumed a tracheotomy would change Beth's course.

Dr. Greer arrived at 5:05 a.m. unshaven and uncombed, assisted by a resident-in-training who would cut a small breathing hole in Beth's neck and insert a tube to relieve her struggle to breathe. To save time he chose to perform the procedure in her bed since she was in a coma and anesthesia would not be required. "Be best if you and Mary step out while we do this."

I was glad to have someone tell me what to do.

In less than fifteen minutes the new breathing tube was in place. We hovered over Beth watching for improvement.

Three hours passed. Mary and I ran out of anything to say. I no longer needed to appear casual for her sake. Hope slid into despair. Little-girl squeals of laughter echoed in my ears. Mary wiped Beth's forehead and face. Beth's chest rose and fell with increasing expansions. Her pulse reached 182 beats per minute on the monitor.

At 9:36 a.m. her blood pressure decreased for the first time from 116/74 to 112/68. I checked her pulse: 152 beats per minute. I counted her breaths by holding my palm on her chest: 40 per minute.

Is this the trend we have been looking for?

I confirmed her respiration rate by keeping my hand on her chest for another 60 seconds: 38 cycles per minute, but shallow and labored. Beth's respiration rate was decreasing for the wrong reason.

To one not in the medical field, the decreasing rate would appear desirable, but medicine trains us to recognize patterns, normal and abnormal. I knew her little heart was failing from fatigue.

Oh, God, no, this is not the trend we want.

For two sleepless days and nights, Mary and I watched helplessly as this horror progressed and our daughter's small body fatigued into exhaustion. Afraid to leave the room, we needed a coach to tell us to leave, stay, or scream. We sat on opposite sides of the bed, each resting a loving hand on Beth's shoulders, holding each other's hand across our daughter's legs forming a triangle. I raised my head to look at Mary, but already she was looking at me with resignation. Tears ran down her cheeks, and I matched them, drop for drop. We cried in silence looking at each other. We never cried together again, unwilling to relive the pain. In a haze, doctors and nurses filtered in and out of the room. Mary and I sat quietly holding the triangle position until Beth took her last breath.

∽

On a gray overcast morning we watched our beautiful daughter die. Her small soul slipped away so quietly. I heard Mary's heart break.

I recall walking to the door and telling those outside something to the effect that there was no more. The attending nurse entered the room, removed the IV, and applied a Donald Duck Band-Aid. She cautiously made eye contact, gave Mary and me consoling hugs and kisses on our cheeks, turned, and left the room.

The gurney could not navigate around the bed without moving furniture. Even at this stage, I needed to take action, feel productive. I lifted our warm, limp, lifeless Beth and cradled her small body in my arms. Mary tucked in the blanket under Beth's arms. After I lay Beth on the gurney, Mary made one last adjustment of the blanket with a neat fold under her chin.

There will never be another tomorrow for me to play with her. This is my final act as her father.

Mary earned the privilege of the last goodbye. She gently cupped Beth's cheeks with both hands and kissed her forehead. "I love you." Her halting whisper held such sorrow I thought her heart might tumble out and fall to her feet. A hard lump lodged in my throat but tears did not come.

My life has been so busy. I have just begun to know Beth. Last year we had four people in the family photo. How do we explain three this year? How to explain the permanence of death to six-year-old Lori?

Medical science and I failed one of my children.

Learning to Climb

Now what?

Where was a coach, a comforting voice over my shoulder telling me what to do? Should Mary and I call on our friends and family who held vigil outside Beth's hospital room? We didn't want well-meaning hugs and soft pats on our backs. We didn't want to answer the what-can-I-do questions. Others could not help us navigate our grief.

There was the first sympathy card from a colleague and the sorrowful face of the always-smiling nurse Lucille who worked in our office. I tried to find my way out of a fog. Someone contacted a funeral home and cemetery. Beth's funeral took place two days later.

Within the first week, a polite man and woman came to our house by appointment. They represented the Communicable Disease Division of the Tulsa City County Health Department. Their job required them to monitor infectious diseases. The four of us gathered at the kitchen table with a pot of coffee. They inquired about our health history, including six-year-old Lori's health, and requested to see all documented immunizations. We then explored every potentially important detail in the critical timeline of events: where we visited with Beth, who was present, what we ate. We appreciated that they were only executing their jobs by collecting data for the public's general health, but, from our perspective, they could have been more sympathetic. They never acknowledged our pain. We might as well have been filling in squares as they performed their duties with dry, clinical diplomacy. The interview pressed us to relive Beth's symptoms, treatment, and death. When they walked out the door, we were drained from any further detailed discussion. Rehash would constitute sawing sawdust.

We outlived our child and had to buy a grave marker. How does one do that?

❧

Every room in our home contained an invisible line between Mary and me that we did not cross. We kept our own thoughts, suffered in silence, hid within ourselves. What I really wished was that we could talk through our tragedy. Instead, our home became a minefield. I grew afraid of staying home, afraid of visiting with Mary, afraid of burying myself in a foxhole of silence.

Guilt riddled me as I weaseled out the front door in search of diversion, working on tenterhooks each day, hiding my sorrow by staying busy. Interacting with others distracted me, dulled the edge, but I left Mary alone to witness one less laughing child to help and hug.

I hurt. I hurt for Mary. I could put my hand over the center of my chest where the pain was most acute. Alone in an elevator or restroom, I placed the palm of one hand on top of the other over my lungs and heart and pushed, pushed hard, as though to squeeze out the pain.

We were out of balance with what were once routine activities. Mary's recipes changed, not in volume, but because of what we could swallow with minimal chewing: soups, macaroni and cheese, mashed potatoes, ice cream. We had already swallowed too much and lost our appetite. Before, when I arrived home from work, my routine was to scuffle with the two girls, sometimes in pillow fights. Other nights I palmed their chests and stomach, hoisting them high above the bed in a moment of giggling melodrama that ended in a fake body slam down to the bed on their backs. Together we played as a team when they squealed and I grunted comments and made faces like the flamboyant wrestler, Gorgeous George. Mary usually admonished us to quit before we damaged the bed. Dynamics of a critical mass of three cannot be replicated with two.

Lori no longer ran and jumped on my lap or my back or hit me with a pillow while standing on a chair by a door. Did she not want to play? Was she giving me space? Months passed before I heard her feminine squeal as she played with neighborhood kids. Lori became the third person in our home never to question or talk about our loss.

Mary fell asleep quickly at night. I resented her sounds of deep sleep, gifting her escape from our loss and leaving me alone to grieve and stare into the dark for hours. Grief morphed first into insomnia, then anger. The injustice of a child's death angered me. My thoughts played over and over: what if, if only, I should have. I went to sleep angry and woke up to the alarm exhausted. Unable to sustain my level of anger without a target, I eventually stopped swinging in the dark.

Mary and I crawled through each day talking in whispers and short sentences. Tension permeated every room, closet, drawer. Surely Mary must have hurt more during the days. In the evenings, her cheeks showed streaks of dried tears. Instead of calling out, "It's me!" when I arrived home, we shared a long silent hug.

We recognized the squirm factor of friends. I'm sure their hearts went out to us, but they didn't know how to connect so they side-stepped around us. Mary and I shared a thorny bed that only time could dull.

From elementary school through graduate school, the mantra by teachers was reduced to the same: get a good education and the world will treat you well. Science had let me down. My education did not prepare me for a black-hole event. My class notes and bookshelves did not contain a single reference about losing a child. I was out in front with no one to charge.

∞

What is the difference between faith and hope? When did I lose faith in medical science and retreat into hope that life would magically get better?

Peers avoided me. They didn't know how to initiate conversation and neither did I. My isolation was self-inflicted. When I saw the children's pediatrician, we said hello, and that was that. We never engaged in discussion. Passing eyes never lingered. I was not ready to hear a joke but craved good eye contact, a smile, or an offer of conversation.

Should I commence a chat to imply that it's okay to talk with me about trivial matters? How about last night's ballgame? Or the upcoming Academy Awards? Please talk to me. Anyone. But conversation could turn into a minefield of unexpected questions and answers, suddenly becoming personal and opening up the pain. I was too vulnerable.

I became an expert in what not to say. Don't you dare tell me, "I know how you feel." The first times I heard that, the shallow statement caught me off guard. How to respond? How the hell can they possibly know? I was ready to punch the next person who said it. One of my peers, a man never at a loss for inappropriate words, said, "No problem, just have another baby."

Slapped off balance and unable to think of an appropriate response, I staggered backward into a chair, feeling like a boxer clobbered in the ring. I faked examining a patient's chart to overcome disbelief. I looked at my watch, the same watch used to count Beth's breathing. My breath mimicked hers: too fast. Memories flashed with original intensity. Like an illusionist who doesn't allow anyone to see his actions, I released the latch on my watch, stood up, walked past my peer, and allowed my watch to slide through my fingers into the trash container unnoticed. I never wore a Bulova again.

Some speak of a mountaintop experience; few mention an abyss. If one has never been in an abyss, there is no reason to learn to climb. I could only hope that being down would make being up sweeter. That is the hand I have been dealt. What of the hours and days to come? How would I use them? Would I watch my life happen or take charge? I began to climb.

My science-oriented education was based on cause and effect and reproducible evidence. Not understanding the cause of Beth's death, I was living through the effect. How to navigate through pain to get to the other side? I needed direction, but found it difficult to follow a compass without knowing how to locate my true north, my stability. Even with a handle on what was right and wrong, I could not get my balance. I had always been driven. Every moment of my conscious life was planned and filled, as though in stopping to gaze at the mountains or listen to a bird, I might cease to exist.

Caring for my patients, I reminded myself, gave me no choice but to go when called. I wanted to be completely devoted to patients and my family, but there were not enough hours. Beth did not experience enough pillow fights or learn how to hide and be quiet; Lori had not yet learned how to swim and build a birdhouse. I had not been present enough in their lives. What lay ahead? I needed to nurture my wife and daughter as well as be a provider. Was there a lesson to be learned? I craved meaning for our loss.

On my way home from work, I often stopped in a park by the Arkansas River to cry and remember Beth. She was almost two years old, just starting to say Da-Da. I had lived fifteen times longer than she. Outliving a child can destroy a marriage. I needed distance, measured distance. Tears streamed down my cheeks and I let myself sob, knowing no one would hear me. I never let Mary, or anyone else, see me grieve.

Mary and I wanted to believe that love transcends grief. We went for counseling with superficial complaints of sex, stress, and work, mentioning Beth only as a passing thought. The counselor couldn't connect the dots.

Without trying to replace Beth, Mary and I brought Amy home from the hospital fourteen months after our loss. New life in our house eased the silence, gave Mary renewed purpose. Lori's voice rang with delight as she doted over her new sister, and I journeyed up from the abyss into heady family relationships I never saw coming.

Once a Soldier

During my junior year at Northeastern State University (NSU) in Tahlequah, Oklahoma, my date and I attended an annual fall Frontier Dance where everyone dressed western. At 11:00 p.m. we closed down the on-campus dance and by tradition moved to a different location off-campus where we would dance to a band until mid-morning.

The after-party took place in Greenleaf Lodge, a large one-room log lodge built in the mid-30s near Muskogee, twenty minutes from NSU. The powdered dance floor led straight to a massive old fireplace. While we waited for the band and other fun-lovers, the door opened and a fellow I kind of knew yelled a loud hoot and ran inside.

As he reached the corner of the dance floor at top speed, he dropped to his side, sliding across the floor like into home plate. He stopped with his feet against the fireplace hearth. I was impressed by the clever entry since the rest of us had only sauntered in. At the moment his feet tagged the hearth, we heard another yell, and a spirited girl followed in his steps, running and dropping to her side, sliding across the floor and stopping next to him. I was even more impressed.

That was the first time I saw Mary. We began dating a month later; our relationship quickly blossomed. We married over the Christmas holidays a year and a half later during my first year of medical school in Kansas City.

༄

Fresh-cut grass fell from my shoes as I walked into the kitchen.

"Feel this," Mary said. She raised her left arm. "There's a knot in my armpit. I haven't noticed it before. It's kinda in my breast and more than a kernel."

I rinsed and dried my hands before spreading my index and middle finger over the lump, measuring its length and breadth, testing its connection to the underlying bone or breast tissue. If the knot didn't move, it was attached to bone and wouldn't be within her breast. It moved. She knew that I knew too much. Any mass in a woman's breast must be considered cancer until proven otherwise. I hoped she didn't see my clenched jaw. A long moment passed before I could untangle my voice. "We should get you in to see Dr. Wilson. He'll probably order a mammogram."

Mary began wiping down the kitchen cabinets. When she finished one, she moved to the next until she completed a full circle, then began again. Thinking it best not to comment on her repetition, I considered giving her a long hug but rejected the idea, fearing physical contact might magnify the issue.

We sat through the *Andy Griffith Show*. Silence roared over the laugh track chuckles, teeth brushing, showering, and going to bed.

I awakened before the alarm. Mary's breathing told me she was awake long before me. Unable to lie quietly staring out the window as light filled the sky, I swung my feet to the floor. "Did you get any rest?"

"So-so. I need to wake up Amy and fix breakfast."

Usually Mary flowed about the kitchen like an experienced chef. Not this morning. She hesitated with her hand on cabinet handles. She stared into the refrigerator.

During breakfast, Amy was her usual middle-school self, scurrying about, talking with toast in her mouth, hopping around on one foot, then the other, while putting on shoes, unaware of our silence. Mary sipped her coffee. I dragged my spoon around in my oatmeal, casting a glance now and then at the kitchen clock. My shirt pocket contained a scrap of paper with Dr. Wilson's telephone number on it. At 7:02 a.m. I paged him from our bedroom. Mary was still sipping her coffee when I returned. "Dr. Wilson said for us to come on over to his office this morning."

"Us? You don't have to go with me. Go take care of your patients. It's okay. Whether you are with me or not won't make any difference in what he has to say."

What I heard was, I will do this by myself.

I stood at the door, reluctant to go to work. "You're going to do just fine," I said. We hugged a normal going-to-work-hug. Alone in my car I could not center the key in the ignition with my shaking hand.

You're going to do fine? What I meant to say was everything is going to be just fine.

The risk factors overwhelmed me: female, age forty-five, breast mass.

∽

At an early age Mary decided that whatever happened or didn't happen in life was her responsibility. Her father left the family when she was six years old. She did not see him again until her college years. With children to support and no formal education, Mary's mother journeyed through unpaid rents and frequent moves as she searched for a path of survival. Mary attended ten schools by the fifth grade. She packed her lunch, walked to school alone, listened in class, learned to make friends quickly, and became an outstanding student, the ideal child soldier. Her grades qualified her for the National Honor Society. She never missed a day of high school. Independence became her identity, and duty outranked discomfort, mental or physical.

∽

Knowing Mary's background, I could not rob her of going to the critical doctor visit by herself, even in the face of what could be a grave prognosis. By not pulling me from my work, she fulfilled her self-imposed responsibility. She lived her independence and made no concessions. Mary said I didn't have to go. That was the way Mary talked. But I should have gone. I made the wrong choice in the kitchen that morning by yielding to her independence at the expense of my responsibility.

My pager went off while I sat in my office looking at a photo of Mary and our girls. With my heart racing, I punched in the numbers.

"Hi, Harold, this is Walt Wilson. Mary just left my office. After viewing her x-rays and feeling several suspicious nodes, I've scheduled her for a mammogram today and biopsy tomorrow. What we do from here will be determined by her test results. I'll review her mammogram at noon. I went over this with Mary and she understands."

"I understand," I said, but I didn't. I only heard frightening words. The conversation must have ended because I hung up, slumped back in my chair, and tried to take a deep breath. Collecting my thoughts, I called the radiology department.

∽

The radiologist and I viewed Mary's x-rays hanging on the view box. "See these speckled areas of increased density, Harold? I have to report this as suspicion of malignancy."

I walked out of his office as a zombie and couldn't recall my own floor number.

∽

Mary wasn't home when I arrived. A note said she was out to the supermarket to stock our house. When she returned with arms full of grocery sacks, I kissed her on the cheek. "Here, let me help you."

"I'm going to have a biopsy in the morning," she said, avoiding eye contact.

"Yeah, I know. Dr. Wilson called and brought me up to date."

We brought in more groceries without eye contact or even casual conversation. I considered saying something stupid to ease the tension, but Mary moved about the kitchen with great ease, probably energized by having a plan for her family.

"The biopsy is at 7:30 a.m. That will give me time to get Amy off to school."

I didn't know what to say in the face of her efficiency. "You're going to do just fine."

She rested her knife on the cutting block and looked into my worried face for the first time. "I know I will." She stared long enough for me to comprehend her declaration, then she chopped up a cucumber for our salad.

Mary and I fumbled through household talk until bedtime. When she turned off her reading lamp, I rolled over to give her a goodnight hug and peck on the cheek, our decades-old ritual. Her cheek was wet. We hugged longer than usual before she rolled onto her side so we could spoon in the dark, both pretending to fall asleep. We watched a full moon out our patio windows as it climbed above the trees, arced across the sky, and settled beyond the horizon. An animal scuffled outside, an owl hooted, a distant train whistle blew long and low night sounds. Mary was listening, but I wasn't sure what she was hearing.

Yearning to give Mary more support and feeling I should have gone with her to that first consultation, I fretted about having abandoned her to receive the horrible news alone. This was new territory. My wife was on a journey without me. Feeling inadequate when we lost our two-year-old Beth twenty years earlier, here I was again at the beginning of another journey. After Beth died, we did not discuss or dissect that event; we turned the page and carried on. Now we had come to a new page, but functioned the same, as if the problem would go away if we didn't talk about it. No matter my rationalizations, guilt stuck on me like superglue.

Mary and I were so busy in our lives, we did not learn to exchange intense personal feelings or discuss her report. We both knew bringing up the subject of cancer meant considering the reality of death.

Duty outweighed Mary's personal concerns as she sent Amy on to school and called Lori at college out of state. "Don't come home. You can't make a difference, except to interrupt your studies. Daddy will call you when I'm finished with the biopsy."

Mary and I agreed with Dr. Wilson that if the biopsy came back positive for cancer, he was to continue with surgery including full breast removal. More lymph nodes with cancer in her armpit would mean more breast tissue needed to be removed. In order to save anesthetic time, I prearranged with Dr. Wilson to call me from surgery with his findings.

Seeing patients during Mary's surgery was more helpful than mindlessly thumbing through magazines in a waiting room. Usually I sat involved with my patients knee to knee, eyeball to eyeball, engaged with their concerns, but not that day.

ᕤᕤ

"Dr. B., you're wanted on the phone."

I excused myself from the patient in front of me, walked with dread to my office and closed the door, steeling myself with three breaths before I picked up the phone. "Hello."

"Mary has cancer in her breast and in many nodes," Dr. Wilson said.

"I understand. I'll honor your decision on how much breast to take," I said and hung up.

My nurse leaned through the doorway. "Dr. B., are you all right? Dr. B.? We still have patients waiting. I could send them home."

"What do you think?"

"No new patients. We know them all. They need x-rays and routine rechecks." She paused. "I think you should see them. Beats staring out that window."

The security of routine helped.

ᕤᕤ

Mary also needed the security of routine on her first postoperative day. "If you bring the checkbook and files from home, I can start paying some bills," she said with a thick tongue while under the influence of pain-killing narcotics.

One week after she left the hospital, I accompanied Mary for her first postoperative visit. Dr. Wilson spoke in soft but direct tones. He talked with her, not at her. "You need to understand that we are not done. There is no way to determine at the surgery table if I got all of the cancer. You will need further consultation with an oncologist, which probably means radiation and chemotherapy. But that will be his call."

Two weeks later, I went with Mary for her first appointment with Dr. McCollough who said, "Based on the location and number of cancerous nodes, I recommend we go after any possible remaining cancer cells. A combination of radiation and chemotherapy gives you the best odds."

I butted in. "Will this make her nauseated?"

"More than nauseated. Either radiation or chemotherapy will make her sick, but combined, I can tell you she will be *real* sick. I can give you medication that may help with the nausea."

"How long will this take?" Mary asked.

"You'll probably need three rounds of chemotherapy. Figure four to six weeks. You're likely to lose your hair, so start shopping for some head scarves and a wig. If you ever wanted to try a different hair style, now is the time."

"When will I know if surgery got all of the cancer?"

"Periodic blood work will tell me. If you can make it to five years, you have a high probability of being cured. If you make it to ten, you are absolutely cured."

"I'm going for ten," she said with a determined voice.

That was the last time I accompanied Mary to a doctor's office. Thereafter she insisted on going alone. We never discussed the subject. I just knew that was what she needed to do.

Mary's concerns for her family outweighed thoughts of vomiting, diarrhea or hair loss. Before her first dose of chemotherapy, she informed me of her plan: "I've made a list for the market and stocked the house with staples. I can do some laundry but will need help changing my sheets more than once a week. That other list in the top drawer under the phone tells you when to pick up the dry cleaning. I'll pay bills between treatments. Also, I've arranged for Amy to ride in a carpool, but keep your beeper charged because she will need a ride now and then."

She nodded for me to follow her into the laundry room as she worked. Guarding her left arm in a sling, she began folding clothes as she explained her thoughts. I watched her fold one shirt twice. She caught what she was doing and looked up at me to see if I was aware of the double fold. When she saw I was, she smiled, shrugged her shoulders and said, "You caught me. By the way, I've picked out a bucket for the side of my bed."

"Anything else I can do?"

"You can share Amy's bathroom with her. I'd like to have a bathroom to myself. I don't know what to expect."

Once again I knew too much. As a surgeon, I witnessed wound infections and recurrences of cancer resulting in dreadful qualities of life.

After her first round of chemotherapy, Mary said, "That's it! I might as well stick that anti-nausea medicine in my butt for all the good it does. Start calling now and find some marijuana. I feel like a dog that's been given worm medicine. Give the dog just enough poison to kill the worms and not quite kill the dog. That's a fine line. I'm no different than a sick dog that crawls under the porch to lick his wounds. I want to be left alone and crawl under the porch. I don't want to be pressed to talk to company and answer how I'm doing. Just push some food and water back to me. I'll come out when I feel better." She paused and made the motion of scissors cutting. "When this is over, cut that bucket into little pieces, make a pile, and burn it."

That was the closest Mary ever came to complaining.

Weeks after the surgery, Lori was home on summer vacation in time to help Mary. "Mom, do you have a bong under the bed? The next time you're going to smoke some medicine, let me know so I can air out the house. Smells like a commune in here. If you can hold it down, I can cook some of that with brownies."

"Thanks, but I'll stick to what I won't throw up."

One day when we were running an errand, Mary rolled down the window to let the wind blow in her face. "My hair is blowing away. I mean *really* blowing away. There goes a wad out the window now. Watch this." Another wad blew out. "I bet that driver behind us thinks we're shaving a goat."

What would I do without her? Thank heavens our girls were old enough to take care of themselves. What about me? I wanted Mary to console me. I needed salve for my heart. When I needed her most to take care of me, she was vomiting. Everything was backwards. I needed comfort for my squeezed heart and no one could apply soothing ointment like Mary. Sometimes the salve consisted of dragging her hand across my shoulders as she passed my chair or sharing a laugh-out-loud scene in a movie. But Mary was going to live. You betcha she was.

Together in the fifties and sixties, we listened to music and learned about romance. Those shared coming-of-age events with testosterone and estrogen boiling could not be duplicated with someone else. If I could think it up, she was for it. We shared good times, lean times, and occasionally heartaches, but never made even a passing acquaintance with boredom.

Mary danced better than anyone I knew. She made me feel like the king of the dance floor, especially when she grinned. She could follow any step, even if I made one up. Male friends told me they always wanted to dance with Mary because she made them look good. When she flashed that grin even now, my knees wanted to buckle and I felt special. Her grin radiated a deep joy. Hearing music of that era, I feel the pull of the dance floor and that grin. I want to do more than tap my foot. I get heady.

Who would feed and take care of me if she were not around?

❧

Ever since Lori was born, we sent out a Christmas card with a family photo reflective of the past year. By September, our family traditionally began fretting and arguing about whose idea was best. Mary made an announcement. "I don't care what we do, but I want to show that I am alive and kicking. If I can survive this experience, I will have broken the stigma of cancer."

We dragged our trampoline from beneath a tree out under a clear sky. The four of us lined up and practiced bouncing, attempting to be in the air simultaneously. The odds of getting everyone at the same height with eyes open and grins on our faces were not good. Capturing the perfect combination was as difficult as photographing four ducks passing overhead with all wings down at the same moment. One of us would go down and spring the next one up. Thanks to a neighbor kid who shot two rolls of film before shooting the perfect frame, Mary made her point. She was alive and kicking, even with a wig.

❧

Fuzz on Mary's scalp returned as a helmet of thick, dark hair without a trace of gray and more bounce than a teenager. She may have come through her ordeal with physical scars but she survived without mental ones. Her old self reappeared with an increased urge to live life to the fullest. "I don't recommend the price," Mary said when I complimented her.

Not day by day nor week by week but month by month we recovered our lives. Over subsequent years, I watched Mary discreetly feel for nodes in her left and right armpits. Those isolated moves evolved into unconscious searches, especially before bedtime. Once, as I turned down the hall, I stopped and watched Mary run her fingers over wall photos of Lori and Amy and our family foursome.

One day she returned from a visit to Dr. McCollough with a big grin. "Five years! My odds are going up. Cancer-free for five years. This was my second goal." I asked about her first goal. "To live long enough to see Lori graduate from college and Amy from high school. Now my third goal is to live cancer-free for ten years."

"Any others?" I asked.

"Yeah, but it's been an on-going goal." Mary paused. "To help you reach your goals."

∽

Too nervous to ask what the original odds were for Mary's survival until after the five-year mark, I trapped Dr. McCollough in the hospital hall. "By the way, I never asked you. What were Mary's odds of survival?"

"With the number of cancerous lymph nodes and their location, she was looking at seventy-five percent."

"Seventy-five percent chance of living?" I leaned forward.

"No, twenty-five percent chance of living. Only one in four patients makes it to five years with her cancer stage."

"Did she know that?"

"Yes."

A sweat-popping moment while his words racked my body. The raven's wing brushed my shoulder and breezed the side of my face. Nauseated within seconds of hearing Mary's odds, I began to feel faint and tightened my stomach muscles to force blood into my head to prevent me from fainting. I slid down the wall, shoulder dragging across the light switch and turning off the room light as I sank into a chair.

I couldn't stop thinking about Mary's strength and dignity. Dignity is self-respect and a sense of self-worth. Without her dignity, she would become a lesser person to herself. Unacceptable. Mary never complained. She never whined. She never stumbled. Now I understood. That was her duty. Once a soldier, always a soldier.

Lori, Mary, Amy, Harold Alive and Kickin'

Ben's Condition

Beep-beep! Beep-beep!
"Marsha," I called out to the circulating nurse, "can you get that page?"

A combination of events delayed a knee ACL reconstruction scheduled for my neighbor's nineteen-year-old daughter until today. Working in a sterile field, I continued preparing the graft, moving the camera about in the patient's knee while watching a monitor. By now Marsha was talking on the wall phone. Keeping a safe distance to avoid contaminating me, she leaned forward and spoke softly through her mask to me, for my ears only.

"Lori's in labor. She's been admitted to the OB floor."

Three weeks earlier, an ultrasound identified the baby about to be born as a boy. Lori and Doug had already chosen the name—Bennett Battenfield Stewart. He would carry on the Battenfield name. A sense of urgency seized me.

Three years earlier, Lori gave birth to twins, Sam and Max. Delivery complications broke Max's arm above his right elbow, stretching the nerve at the fracture and causing wrist paralysis. Both Lori and her husband, Doug, were physicians, Lori in industrial medicine and Doug in pediatrics. With their shared history, they knew too much regarding potential complications. Though unwritten protocol implied I was too close to the patient as the grandfather, they wanted me to take care of him. In two decades as an orthopedic surgeon, I had never addressed such an injury. Colleagues had no advice to offer or experience to share. The literature reported isolated cases; the only recommendation was to splint his entire arm with his wrist cocked up for four weeks and hope for the best. I applied a splint cast and the fracture healed within one month, but Max could not straighten his wrist until after the end of three long months. Finally, I slept all night.

∽

Unable to always be with Mary during difficult times, I especially wanted to be with her and Lori one floor up and less than fifty feet away. Everyone in the surgery worked in punishing slow motion. A tingling sweat broke out across my back, then raced down my buttocks and the backs of my legs. My heart pounded. *Is this shock?* While all eyes watched the monitor, I bumped my camera-holding hand against that of the surgical resident and transferred instruments. He took the camera and continued the surgery.

Beep-beep! Beep-beep! Marsha crossed the room. "Lori's in delivery."

I couldn't shake my concern. As surgery approached completion under my supervision, I made plans for a quick exit and whispered to the resident, "I'm going to leave when we get the last suture in. After you get the dressing and splint on, I want you to write the orders and visit with the family. Got it?" Slowly I stepped back from the table, removed my gown, gloves, and mask, and delivered the routine exiting statement to the surgical crew: "Thanks, folks." Grabbing my long white coat, I hustled down the hall past two surgery rooms to the stairwell and exploded up the stairs to the obstetric floor. Pausing outside the waiting room to catch my breath and inhale false bravery, I entered.

∽

Mary sat on the edge of a chair, her lips quivering as she leaned forward. "Lori's got troubles." I sat down. "Doug is with her in the delivery room. Ben developed respiratory distress just before delivery, and it's too late for a C-section."

Doug's parents, David and Mary Stewart, eyed me from across the room. With my game face screwed on tight, I leaned back, crossed my legs and cupped my hand around my right knee, wanting to appear calm and in control, secretly feeling my pulse with my right thumb on my left wrist. *Fifty beats in thirty seconds. No wonder I feel woozy.* I blew out my breath and kept my voice modulated. "How is Lori doing?"

"I told you." Mary swept her hand, palm down above her lap, indicating no more questions.

Although I have been on this side of a surgical door before, practice didn't ease the anxiety. "What time did she go in?"

"I don't know."

"About how long has she been in delivery?"

Mary chopped the air with her hand. That's enough, her hand stated again.

A window curtain fluttered above the air conditioning vent. The TV was muted. Doug's parents stared at the floor, Mary stared at the door waiting for anyone to come in, and I stared at the clock whose second hand was moving forward when nothing else in our universe was.

"What time is it?"

Mary looked up at the wall clock but not me. "One twenty five."

At last, Lori's obstetrician stood before us in the waiting room. "Lori is doing fine. She is one tough lady. Due to the prolonged delivery, the baby is in the nursery where we will need to watch him very closely. His post-delivery rating is not the best."

Strange he did not sit and discuss details with us. Mary and I went to see Lori and Doug in her post-delivery room.

"They brought Ben to me, but he can't nurse," Lori said.

An awkward silence descended over the room, unspoken words piled high. Doug caressed Lori's arm. "They took him to the nursery for oxygen," Doug said.

Ben isn't right. Hours passed. Minutes maybe. Back in the waiting room, I slipped away to the nursery. Swaddled in a light blue blanket, Bennett Battenfield Stewart was a beautiful baby boy with a full head of dark hair. He weighed in at seven pounds, twelve ounces, a good all-round healthy weight. He lay quiet and inert as I picked him up. Tears filled my eyes. Sitting in a rocker, I hugged him higher in my arms, kissed his forehead and each closed eye. He smelled new like a baby should. The easy rocking gave me solace. Off to one side, the nursery nurses watched me closely but dropped their heads when I looked up. The head nurse granted me a few minutes of holding Ben, then, without saying a word, lifted him from my arms. I never saw his newborn dark blue eyes. If I could hold Ben for only a brief time, how much worse must it be for Lori and Doug?

❧

Gripped with a desire to set my eyes on the place where Ben's troubles began, I left the nursery to look for answers in the empty delivery room. A single folded white sheet lay on the table in the center of the room waiting to drape the next mother. There were no signs of a struggle. We all realized Ben needed more time. The history of healing has always been waiting and allowing more time. Six of us talked amongst ourselves, convincing one another that tomorrow would show improvement.

Mary and I slept a few hours at home with thoughts pushed deep under our pillows. In the morning we left before sunup in such a hurry I forgot to shave and looked like a new father after a long delivery. Mary's hair hung limp.

With shoulders slumped from fatigue, Doug sat next to Lori in her room, waiting for another consultation. Doug's parents sat with us for a while but eventually excused themselves to care for the twins. Four hours dragged past. The intensive care pediatrician entered the room with a status report. We were expecting a progress report: big difference. He chose his words carefully. "Ben is breathing well on his own, but his reflexes don't respond appropriately. All he needs at present is a feeding tube." *The pediatrician is dancing around the issue. Ben's reflexes aren't working; he's in a coma.*

Fear turned to grief in seconds. The walls swayed like weeds at the bottom of the ocean. I was nauseated, paralyzed, and could not tolerate my daughter hurting. Doug remained calm and supported Lori. Lost in the left corner of her bed, Lori sat with hands wrapped about her knees. As Doug talked, she dropped her feet off the bed and reached for his hand. They spoke in subdued tones.

In the waiting room Mary and I spent the rest of the day talking in positive terms, trying to coach each other. We watched parents and families laughing and glowing as they took a new baby home. Each joyful family sharpened the contrast with ours, with Lori and Doug's distress.

❖

The next day Lori walked about her room and halls for exercise and occasionally looked out the window with me. I was drawn to look west at the slow-running, predictable Arkansas River I had gazed upon unfocused one generation earlier. *Déjà vu.* The timeless river had given me fleeting comfort when we lost Beth, but not today. Today it was an insult.

Physicians explained batteries of laboratory tests. Results were consistent: no change. Yet we held onto irrational hope. As news of Ben's condition spread, family and friends backed away and left us alone to grieve. Another neurologist provided his findings. "Ben is breathing well and receiving adequate nutrition through a gastric tube. As you know, he was oxygen-deprived from the long delivery, and you have been advised to watch and wait. There are no indications for medications or further testing. With his condition, improvement would have been noted within the first day or two. Since he hasn't shown any by now, none can be expected."

❖

Ben's condition is permanent. What is his life expectancy? Days, weeks or even months?

Physician consultations mentioned only a limited life expectancy. I worried how Lori would tolerate holding Ben, a comatose baby who could not nurse, and how Mary and I would respond to questions about our grandchildren. My network of colleagues provided an overload of information without solutions. What were we to do now? Who could advise us?

Day four passed. On the fifth day, Lori and Doug processed options with attending physicians: locate an institution for permanent care, leave Ben in the hospital, or take him home. Sequestered in the privacy of her room, they struggled with a decision no parent should have to make. I ached to carry all or any part of their burden. Rotating between my office next door, the hospital cafeteria, the waiting room, and Lori's room, I tried to see my orthopedic patients but was unable to focus on their complaints. Lori and Doug's decision would shape the future of our family.

Doug entered the waiting room and faced Ben's four grandparents. "We are going to take Ben home, care for him ourselves as long as possible, and decide from there. Lori and I will develop a schedule to feed him through his stomach tube. Lori is on maternity leave, and we will learn as we go."

With that declaration, Lori and Doug became our heroes. Ben was a loved child regardless of his disability. The decision surprised us, not by its character but by the level of responsibility they were assuming. In addition to Ben, they needed to care for their three-year-old twins.

∾

Through the anguishing years of Beth's death and Mary's cancer, guilt weighed on my shoulders like a sack of rocks that grew heavier each year. I wished I had been more supportive. Now was a chance to redeem myself in my own eyes.

I followed Doug into the nursery where he began preparing Ben to go home. "I want to be placed on the feeding schedule for Ben." Doug acknowledged my request with a single nod.

Mary would assist in caring for the twins, and Doug's parents, living in Skiatook, would help her as much as possible. We would work as a family. Doug determined the schedule and the amount of liquid nutrition. The around-the-clock feeding, turning, and diaper changes began. Because Doug was a pediatrician, recording fluid intake, urine output, and oral nutrition in a log was second nature.

By the middle of the third week at home, Ben's heart rate increased. His breathing became more labored and his urine output was decreasing. We knew the meaning of these signs. Doug and Lori asked me to tell the extended family that they did not want a formal funeral but cremation, followed by a graveside service with only the immediate family.

On Thursday I visited the Ninde Funeral Home and explained the situation. I expected a handshake and straightforward instruction, but the funeral director placed a caring hand across my shoulders and invited me to sit beside him on a bench. When Ben died, I was to bring my grandson wrapped in a blanket and they would take care of him from there. I told Lori and Doug of my visit. "If I am not here, don't move Ben, just call me. Is that okay?" They simply nodded. I was determined to shoulder all non-critical decisions. They couldn't. I could.

We never used the words "die" or "dead." Our conversations were in medical terms which distanced us from personal events. We knew Ben would soon die and I would be the one they called to pick him up. I could not stop his death but could change my role in the family by being more present. Never having plowed this field before, I didn't know where the buried stumps were.

I decided to take another step to shield Lori and Doug from further stress. Although Doug was also a Tulsa County Medical Examiner, the family was not exempt from following the law. Without their knowledge, I called the police department on Friday and advised someone named Roy of the circumstances. "Do we need a witness?" Roy assured me we were now on record of the pending event with a defined funeral home and paper trail. When death occurred, I was to notify his office to satisfy their records. His empathy surprised me, gave me a measure of comfort from a stranger.

The following Tuesday Doug gave me a status report as we changed feeding shifts. "Ben's temperature is going up along with his heart rate, and his diaper has been dry the last three changes." We made no eye contact. I heard the report and knew.

∽

The dreaded call could come as a beep on my pager and announce to the world that Ben was dead, so I selected a more private option on my pager: vibration. When it began vibrating that Wednesday afternoon, I felt a cold shadow creep over me and knew my time to take action was at hand. Thank goodness the twins were at home with Mary. The vibrations on my hip felt long and heavy with sadness. I dialed my daughter's home.

"Daddy, it's that time."

The light dimmed in my soul. Again my daughter experienced terrible news about Ben because she was the one determining her baby's last breath. I uttered my rehearsed line. "I'll be right there, honey."

Doug was already home. He and Lori sat at the kitchen table with surrendering shoulders, not talking, no coffee. Both gazed unfocused out the driveway window. Lori's eyes were outlined in red from crying, swollen from fatigue. Doug's exhaustion showed in a two-day beard. Even his clothes looked tired.

I walked behind them and drew my hand across their shoulders. "I'm here. Don't move or say anything. I will take over." My composure was barely skin-deep.

Ben's room was at the top of the stairs. Everything was so quiet. Removing the feeding tube from Bennett Battenfield Stewart, I wiped him with a fresh cloth, applied a fresh diaper, and wrapped him in the blue baby blanket kept in a box in my car trunk for this day. To save Doug and Lori the anguish of cleaning up, I hid the supplies in a drawer, intending to return and clean them out later. From the upstairs phone, I called the police department and asked for Roy. "This is Harold Battenfield."

"Our thoughts are with you, Harold. The police department wishes your family well."

I chose not to go through the kitchen but let myself out the back door. Although my steps were hurried and my heart slammed inside my chest, I slowed before walking past the kitchen window where Lori and Doug sat at the table. I could not ignore them watching me walk past with a bundle that belonged to them. Reluctant to make eye contact, I gave a weak goodbye wave. I think Doug nodded; Lori leaned forward and watched her son disappear from view. Their agony could not have been more obvious if they were bleeding on the floor.

How to place Ben in my car? In the back seat by himself or next to me on the passenger side? Why, of course, he will make this ride buckled up front next to Papa.

I carried Ben into the funeral home without ceremony. Details blurred. Did someone say I was expected? Maybe nothing was said. Did I really hand Ben over so easily? After delivering so precious a package, I gave myself permission to be overwhelmed with fatigue. Someone ushered me to a low chair. Wistful funeral music permeated the air. Someone helped me out the side door.

The pain of Ben's death ambushed me at the curb; profound emotional pain was my buried stump. I walked past my car twice before recognizing it. Fumbling with keys, I collapsed in the driver's seat and let out a sorrow-drenched howl. Thinking someone might hear me and offer to help, I moved my car to the corner of another parking lot to sob for what could have been. From deep within, an elemental force struggled to emerge. Conflicts held back for two generations let loose. Having taken an important role in this family crisis allowed me to feel and witness the pain of the moment as well as past ones, and, thus, to forgive myself.

ᘒ

Instead of driving straight home, I headed for that old Arkansas River. The meandering current is not influenced by those of us struggling with life or death issues, but it has the ability to carry away our grief along with sediment and pollution. A fresh rain in its unlimited tributaries cleanses the river. Grief may require many rains or perhaps, in my case, many seasons.

At the park, I leaned against the roof of my car, testing uncertain legs. To my relief they held. Mesmerized by the winding waters, my breathing slowed and deepened. I walked down to the same spot I visited when Beth died. Four small flat rocks at my feet pleaded to be skipped.

I skipped the first. "Thank you for the months Beth was with us." I skipped the second. "Thank you for Mary's recovery and amazing strength." I skipped the third. "Thank you for the days Ben was with us."

Holding the fourth rock in the crook of my index finger and thumb and leaning far to my right to hurl it as flat as possible across the water, I snapped my wrist at the end of the throw like I did as a boy at my daddy's side. My internal clock began to reset itself. "Thank you for helping me learn how to become the man I want to be."

When the rock settled beneath the surface, I walked uphill unburdened and resolved never again to be in a position to say I wish I had with my family.

ல்

Ben lived thirty-seven days. Lori and Doug never complained, whined or blamed—just like their role model: Mary, my wife, Lori's mother. One year after Ben died, Lori gave birth to Jack.

Amy and Kevin welcomed three children born after Ben: Lauren Battenfield King, Keegan Battenfield King, and Grant Battenfield King.

Both daughters, Lori Anne and Amy Sue, went to court and replaced their middle names with Battenfield. They never asked me. They never told me. Years passed before I accidentally discovered the change.

A GRANDFATHER BREAKS THE CODE

Internal Clock

At five years old our first grandkids approached a rite of passage—learning to ride a bicycle. As the grandfather who had resolved never to be in a position to say I wish I had with my family, I envisioned the fraternal twins, brown-eyed Sam and blue-eyed Max, peddling and yelling with joy. In preparation I purchased a fourteen-inch bicycle at a garage sale for $5.00. The seller threw in a beat-up bright yellow helmet with lightning bolts drawn above each ear and "Susie" lettered in bright red across the back. When Sam and Max revealed their interest in learning to ride, they surely would never notice the girl's name.

One Saturday morning the boys watched "Rugrats" ride a bicycle on our TV.

"Sam, would you like to learn to ride a bicycle like that?" No response. "Max, how about you?" I stood in front of the TV. "Well, would you?"

"Would we what?" Sam said without looking up at me.

"Would you like to learn to ride a bike?"

"Yeah, okay," he said, not taking his eyes off the screen.

He was very interested.

Lori knew I looked forward to teaching them to ride. With mild spring weather in the forecast, she agreed to leave them with me the next Saturday morning without telling them why.

I oiled the chain on the garage-sale bike, aired the tires, lowered the seat, and went inside to find Mary. "I'm going to teach Sam and Max how to ride a bicycle tomorrow."

"You sure they're ready?" she said, tilting her head.

"Yeah, they told me so the other day."

Our half-circle driveway sloped gently down to the street, the perfect place to learn to ride a bike. A kid could start down the slope, turn left at the street, another left back up the slope, and start over again.

◌◌

Because the twins were anxious to learn, on Saturday morning I gobbled down breakfast, scanned the paper, and sipped my too-hot coffee. When Lori dropped them off, the bike was already lined up on the driveway, pointed downhill, training wheels adjusted with a small amount of lean to make a turn, kickstand down, ready for some kid, any kid. I reminded myself they had internal clocks, and I didn't want to push.

I planned to march ahead of them like a drum major through the house to the driveway and waiting bicycle. For sure when they saw the bike, they would break into a run to be the first one on it.

Just as Lori was dropping off the twins, the telephone rang.

"I'll meet you guys outside by the garage," I said.

After the call, the boys were nowhere to be seen outside. Back in the house they had made a detour to the living room and clicked on Saturday morning cartoons. They slumped on the couch, bodies and souls sucked into the TV screen. My agenda had been derailed. We were in conflict before the bike lesson even began.

"Mary, could you help me herd these guys outside?"

She turned off the TV.

"What?" Max bolted up.

Sam looked at me. "What did we do?"

"Nothing. It's what we're going to do. Follow me, boys."

With looks of resignation they fell in behind me out to the driveway and bike in all of its disheveled splendor. "Ready, Max?"

"Where's my bike?" Sam said.

"That's your bike."

Max looked at me. "Then where's my bike?"

"That's your bike."

Max drifted into the garage and returned with duct tape. "I'm going to tape over 'Susie.'"

"Okay, okay, Max, just get on! I'm going to run along and hold you. Sam, wait right here and watch. You'll get your turn. Nana is going to get this on video. You'll look at this video someday and laugh."

Max mounted the seat, gazed down the slope, and sighed. "I want Sam to go first."

"You'll do just fine. I've got you. You can't fall. Just start pedaling."

Overinflated tires on a well-oiled bike roll easily downhill. Max pedaled with more energy than I expected, as though he wanted to get his lesson over with. I controlled his balance, but running stooped while holding the low seat delivered an unwelcome surprise: fatigue by the time we reached the bottom of our slight hill. Training wheels should hold him up, I reasoned, and let go of the seat.

Max didn't yet know how to balance, so he leaned toward my side for support. The left training wheel bottomed out. He continued in a slow left turn until the bike coasted across the lawn and struck a tree, which turned the front wheel at a right angle. Ankles over elbows, he ensnarled himself with the bicycle for a remarkable part-flip, part-roll. He rallied with a mouth full of grass and eyes filled with tears. "I'm done!" he said and sat down by the garage as far away from me as possible.

"I got it!" Mary said, looking through the camera's viewfinder. "That's going to make a great opening scene."

Straddling the crooked wheel and twisting the handlebars back into alignment, I returned the bike to the bottom of the slope. Sam watched with a doubtful expression.

"Okay, Sam, we've learned not to start on a hill, so we're going to start down here. Just get on. I know how to keep up this time."

He looked back at Max. "Do you want another turn?" Max shook his head.

Able to keep up even though my back was killing me, I tried running in a squatted position to give my back a rest, willing to look stupid if only it worked. Sam peddled the circle twice, continuing to rely on the training wheels. As long as those wheels held up the bicycle, the kids could not learn balance, so I removed them.

"Okay, Max, your turn again. I'm going to hold you by your collar so I don't have to stoop over." Apparently, he had resigned himself to tolerating me again. With my right hand I wadded up his collar to get a safe grasp. "Just pedal, honey. I've got you."

Max watched his feet pedal while I looked ahead. Run, run, pedal, pedal. We made it to the street but he began turning right, away from me, so I hauled left, wrenching his shirt high enough to choke him. Once more in tears, he focused on trying to breathe.

"Just give it one more try." I unbuttoned his top shirt button and again held him by his collar. When he started falling, his shirt cleared his throat and chin but pulled over his eyes.

"My turn's over, Papa."

We pushed the bicycle back to the garage.

"Sam, one more turn for you."

He pouted at Mary, searching for relief.

Downcast postures proved the twins didn't each want a bike; in fact, they already had one too many. At last Sam relented and, straddling the bike, removed his helmet to confirm that tape still covered "Susie."

Back to square one; I held the back of the seat. Stoop run, pedal, stoop run, pedal. Sam's wobbles began to exaggerate, expanding into weaves until he cut in front of me. Down we went in the street. He fell first, then me over him and the bicycle. I staggered to a standing position, blood dripping from my left elbow, glasses jammed crooked over one ear and beneath the other. Sam's knee was skinned, as were my left elbow and forehead. Okay, I thought, if they're not ready to balance, I can teach them to brake.

Max was up again. "Max, when I say stop, just push backwards on the pedal." With me grasping the bicycle seat, we picked up speed for better balance, just enough for me to transition from a fast walk to a trot. "Okay, Max. Stop."

He stopped the only way he understood, by removing his feet from the pedals and planting them firmly on the ground with knees locked. He stopped in less than half of one of my strides. Tumbling forward over his left foot, I clung to my only anchor—his bicycle seat—and pulled him over on top of me. Now my knees were skinned.

"Why don't you guys go watch 'SpongeBob SquarePants.'" I eyed Mary and the video camera. "You can just tape over today's lesson."

"You know they aren't ready to ride, don't you?"

"Aw, they'll be looking forward to the next lesson."

For days after the lesson, I examined patients with my left elbow close to my side, hiding superficial injuries. My scabs gradually healed and so did my wounded ego. I mulled over the results of my teaching experiment. Two issues became apparent: I was not as good a teacher as I had imagined, and Mary had been right—the boys weren't ready. Making a contract with myself not to bring out the bike again until they were ready, I leaned it against lawn tools in the garage.

For five months I fretted and searched for answers. The city library contained rooms of how-to books and VHS tapes and yet not one word about how to ride a bicycle. Friends were no help. Maybe riding a bicycle is determined by our DNA and ranks up there with how babies know how to suckle and birds know how to make a nest—they just know. An Internet link implied anyone asking the question wouldn't understand the answer.

How to avoid repeating my mistakes? The teacher must trot fast enough to generate a balancing speed. If the kids were on wheels, their teacher should be, too. I simply needed an equalizer.

Retrieving my ancient rollerblades from the attic, I dusted them off and hid them by my workbench, waiting for dark. Otherwise, I might be pressed to explain my activities to a neighbor. Or Mary.

Mary walked out with the trash, saw the bike leaning against the garage wall, and discovered me lacing up my rollerblades. She pinned me with a steely-eyed look. "What's the bike doing out this time of night?"

"But ... "

"But what?" She swatted down my idea and followed up with a back of her hand to her forehead.

"But I can explain."

"You make a living fixing up people who do such things. You're old enough to know better. This will rank up there with your top ten worst ideas."

"I understand," I said, looking away. "Sometimes I wonder about my ideas, too, especially the ones I've never told you about." Turning face to face, I continued, "Tell you what. I'll make a sharp stick for you to hang in the garage. Next time I get out of line with an idea, you go get that stick and poke me in the eye."

"Sounds as reasonable as some of your ideas."

I unlaced my rollerblades.

When Mary left for Walmart, the bike and I went for a practice run, but even without a rider, I had to run stooped over holding onto the rear of the seat, tilting the bike to the left or right to command a turn. I puzzled over how to control the turns without killing my back. The handle of an old broom wedged behind the seat down through the triangle to rest on the axle between the pedals might do the trick. Holding the broom below the straws, I walked about the driveway, leaning the bike left and right, controlling the turns, even making a circle, then impressed myself with a figure-eight while holding the bike away from me and running upright. *Shazam, Captain Marvel!*

I cut off the old broom behind the seat and went berserk with duct tape, applying it at all points of contact of broom to frame and covering the top of the stick with a significant knob of tape. Satisfied, I rolled the bike into the garage to wait until the twins were ready to learn. Over the summer, the twins would certainly be exposed to other kids riding bikes.

While I was at it, I placed another broom in my workbench vice and twisted it with a pipe wrench until it broke into a section with a long sharp spiral point. I drilled a hole in the blunt end for a lanyard and spray painted the stick bright red. In bold black letters I printed "Mary's Eye Sticker" down one side. It hangs from the garage wall in obvious sight. Mary has never removed it, but the visual reminder is ever present when my mind begins wandering.

∽

One late summer evening I pushed the twins on our giant outdoor swing. "Any kids riding bikes in your neighborhood?"

"Yeah, bunches," Max said.

"Sam?"

"Yeah, just like Max said."

"Max, would you be interested in trying to learn again?" He gave an anemic nod. Sam looked toward Max who shrugged. He hadn't said no.

"Great. I'll pick you both up Saturday and take you to a special place to learn."

∽

We drove to an empty school parking lot. The weather was severe clear with zero wind. After my failed attempt in the spring with one bike and helmet, I purchased a second garage-sale bike, both now outfitted with brooms. All three of us wore used helmets, gloves, elbow and kneepads, looking more like gladiators than bicycle riders, and I wasn't even going to ride.

"Okay, Sam, you go first."

"Papa, make Max go first," Sam said.

"Sam, you go ahead. You already have your helmet on."

Beginning with a fast walk along Sam's left side, I broke into a trot. Sam wobbled and watched his feet while I balanced the bike with the duct-tape knob and looked ahead. He began weaving left into my path. I gently pushed the steering stick to the right, correcting his balance. Wobble, pedal, wobble, pedal.

Hypnotized by his pedaling feet as though they belonged to someone else, Sam and his balance improved, but whenever he looked up, he stopped pedaling. After several laps across the parking lot, we returned to Max.

"Max, it's your turn. Okay?" I said, catching my breath.

Max imitated Sam, eyes on his feet as he rode. Watching neighborhood kids ride bicycles wasn't enough.

"Look up, Max. Look straight ahead." He glanced up for only a second before his eyes returned to his feet. His balance improved, but he didn't have the foggiest idea where he was heading. We approached an island where Sam leaned against a tree. Exhausted, I stopped Max at the curb ten feet short of the tree, fell to my knees and rolled on my back in the grass gasping for air. Max walked over to sit with Sam in the shade. I crawled into the shade with them, and they watched me rest.

A few more rotations on their bikes and balance improved, as did their technique. They started with one foot on a curb and stopped with brakes but still watched their feet. With no idea where they were going or what lay ahead, they may as well have been bungee jumping in the dark.

"Let's try something different. Since you can start on your own, I'm going to run in front of you. Keep your eyes on my back." Max started riding with me running just far enough ahead to keep from being run over. I glanced back, yelling over my shoulder. "Good boy, Max. Watch me, watch me."

A gentle turn to the right, then straight ahead, followed by a gradual turn to the left: Max followed me like a caboose on a train. He stopped watching his feet. Too excited to rest, I ran past Sam and pointed toward Max. "Sam, can you follow me like this?"

"Sure," he said, as if he had done it hundreds of times.

I needed water and a long rest, but bringing water never crossed my mind, focused as I was like a plow horse with blinders.

With Sam watching my back, I ran straight ahead and began gentle turns, all the while yelling, "Good, Sam. Follow me. Stay with me. Good boy." Stumbling down next to Max, I waved Sam on. "Keep going across the parking lot. Turn and come back."

"Papa, Papa, Papa, watch me!" Sam shouted.

"Papa, Papa, my turn, my turn!" Max shouted.

Sam made his last turn grinning wide enough to show off all twenty baby teeth. Max imitated Sam's ride and returned beaming like he had swallowed the sun. He stopped in front of me and balanced himself with both feet on the ground. "I want to go show Mama and Daddy."

I jumped up punching the air with both fists like Rocky Balboa. "We did it!"

The difference between work and play? Doesn't matter. Mistakes? Duly noted. The twins thought our success was all about them, but it was really all about me, the grandfather who learned to adapt his curriculum to his students, the one with an internal clock in sync with his grandkids at last.

Sam, Harold, Max

Harold and His Bike on a Stick

Deleting Fear

A lightning bolt brightened the sky. An early May afternoon storm bent trees and sent a random trash can tumbling across our yard and down the street as the unstable weather front moved along its traditional direction in Oklahoma, northwest to southeast, ushered along by thunder, wind, and rain.

"Hey, kids, let's go out on the porch," I said. "I want to show you something special. You're going to like this."

A small river flooded our lawn; the sweet fragrance of rain infused the air. With Max and Sam snuggled on either side of me and Jack on my lap, we huddled on a front porch bench protected by three walls of the house. No one spoke as driving rain passed in waves from left to right.

The sky exploded with multiple lightning bolts that appeared wired together by a mad scientist. Max and Sam pointed to the explosions, flinched and grimaced at first, unsure how to receive the resulting thunder, then broke into smiles. Four-year-old Jack sat motionless with eyes open wide in fear, watching his older brothers' reactions. At first he smiled reluctantly, but following several loud booms, fell in line.

"Listen for thunder over there," I said leaning forward. Anticipating the approaching rumble, I wrapped my arms two notches tighter around Jack.

"Smell that?" I said. "That's the smell of rain."

"What's rain smell like?" Sam said as he tilted his head back and sniffed the air. Max and Jack tilted their heads back for a whiff of whatever they were missing.

The thought had never crossed my mind before, but they needed an answer. "Maybe earthy or fresh. All I know is rain cleans out the haze and leaves a clear sky."

I relished the role of the instructing grandfather, explaining how we would see lightning from a distance and seconds later hear thunder rolling toward us. But a hidden agenda lurked behind my words. Early activities with our kids and grandkids were often disguised as play, just like today. I wanted their curiosity to prevail over fear in new activities and environments before fear gained a toehold.

"Begin counting the seconds from the flash until you hear thunder. One mile takes about one second. Two miles, about two seconds. We'll count like this: one, one thousand; two, one thousand; three, one thousand, until we hear the thunder. Count the seconds when we see the next lightning. Okay?"

With eyes wide, they nodded and grinned. A lightning flash. "One, one thousand; two, one thou ..." KERRACK!

Expecting thunder to come from the direction of the lightning, it startled us when the clap broke immediately over our heads. Air compression hurt our ears; we recoiled in unison. I ducked with a grunt. The blast startled us so much that I didn't hear the kids' responses and was glad the fading rumbles hid my grunt.

"Wasn't that a pretty sound?" I said with a forced calm voice, snuggling my grandkids closer to me.

"Are you four kids crazy?" Mary said, sticking her head out the front door. "The weatherman just pointed out a string of thunderheads heading our way with heavy rain. He said the rain will be past us in about an hour."

"We're dry and out of the weather." I extended my arms around Max and Sam. "No problem."

The kids looked at Mary who shrugged her shoulders. "Whatever."

The sky again drew dark. Heavy raindrops began pelting the roof. Thunder clapped in the distance; I could tell from our counting that the front was moving our direction. As opposed to weather in other states where overcast skies and drizzle can last for days, spring storms in the Great Plains of Oklahoma usually offers a quick onset, fast pace, and duration measured in hours. Low turbulent clouds roiling overhead can make one want to duck his head beneath them to see at a distance through a green haze. Dramatic lightning, towering thunderheads and bursts of roaring wind leave behind an artist's palette of sunlight and clearing skies.

I wanted to seize this opportunity on the porch to guide the kids through a new experience and break out on the other side of fear, to expose them to a beautiful part of nature rather than watch them develop a phobia to it. My voice and choice of words needed to be soothing and spawn a feeling of lasting comfort, with or without my presence.

∽

During another afternoon spring thunderstorm, I pulled down the folding attic ladder in the garage ceiling. This time four-year-old Lauren joined us. The shallow pitched roof allowed me to stand upright only in the center of the attic. Never having been up there before, the kids explored the cozy space with wonder. Since the only chair in the attic wobbled on three legs, as someone had never gotten around to gluing the fourth, I sat on a Christmas decoration box with Jack. The twins sat on a snow sled, and Lauren rested on a chainsaw case. I surveyed their faces. "Let's turn off the light. Okay?"

Concerned that any one of them could blurt out words of fright, leading to a stampede down the ladder, I needed to assess their willingness to go along with me. If we could cross the first few minutes together in the dark, we would be over the hump. The transition to absolute darkness could be a critical point of deleting fear. "Max, would you go down, turn off the light switch, and come back up and join us?"

Scattered thin rays of light seeped through two air vents, enough light for Max to find his way back to his perch but not enough for us to move around. We sat in the dark, listening to the downpour while lightning flashed through the vents. We waited for thunder. Driving rain kettle-drummed on the roof inches from our heads and washed away the outside world. Last week we enjoyed the earthy aroma of fresh rain, but this week musty attic smells outranked any freshness.

Wanting to feel thunder shaking the roof. I stood rigid, hands flat against the underside of the roof, elbows and knees locked to embody the impact. Tremors traveled in undulating waves through my hands, down my body, and out my feet. For a few exciting seconds, my body was a conduit for a force of nature. Over the years, I had felt the compression on my ears and body but never traveling through my body in a linear pattern. I had never read, heard or seen such, even in a movie. Surely I wasn't the first to experience nature in this way.

Lauren reached out in the dark, found my hip, and hooked her index finger in my belt loop. "Papa," she said with a weak voice, "you're not leaving, are you?"

"No, honey, I'm staying right here with you. To have fun."

As our eyes adjusted to the available light, we could see each other's faces and expressions. Sam stood up next and hesitantly placed his hands under the roof. Max, not to be outdone, jumped up and raised his hands to the roof. Lauren released her finger from my belt loop and joined Jack as they scrambled to a spot where they could reach the roof. The kids looked at one another to see if anyone would chicken out. Nobody did. They locked elbows and knees and, with pressed hands beneath the roof, grinned while they waited for the next flash and the shuddering thunder.

"Wow, did you feel that?" Max whispered.

"Make it happen again, Papa!" Jack shouted.

The feel of thunder was a first for me, but better still, I shared an original experience with my grandkids.

"Isn't this fun?" Lauren whispered to Sam who nodded without changing his position.

Suddenly the single attic light came on and Mary's head entered the attic. "What's happening up here? Looks like everyone is holding up the roof."

"We're waiting for thunder," Sam said.

"Oookay." Mary surveyed and digested the scene. "But you look like a bunch of nuts."

I paused for a moment waiting to be scolded, and the kids stood quietly holding up the roof, following my lead.

"You kids should be reading *Harry Potter*," Mary said.

"Yeah, and with a flashlight," Max yelled in the silence between claps.

"I'll be right back." Mary descended the ladder.

The attic light went off, plunging us back into darkness.

After Mary delivered the book and flashlight, I held the flashlight while the twins alternated reading paragraphs. The drama played out as we sat huddled on makeshift seats, our feet resting on attic beams. Witches and wizards and Harry Potter rode brooms to the rhythm of the rain, while lightning created shock waves that shook the attic around us. Hollywood could not have built a better movie set, including the musty attic smell.

Standing in line with Jack as the last two to descend the ladder, I cupped his face, kissed him on his forehead, patted him twice on the dome of his head, dragged my hand down the back of his head and neck, and gave him a hug across his shoulders just like my mother did to me. All five of us kids climbing down the ladder were different from the ones who had climbed up.

Excited grandkids ran into the house to tell Mary about their adventure. Playing with them, I enjoyed a keen sense of life, death, and immortality. Our grandkids passed over the threshold of a new experience unafraid. After the drama ended, I took time to reflect and question myself.

A month later, Sam called me and was so excited his voice danced over the phone. "Papa, I just wanted to tell you that last night I was lying in bed and heard the prettiest thunder."

Glue Sticks & Guns

As a child, I loved to create hideouts with chairs in the middle of the kitchen. Blanket walls and dim light created an air of intimacy and secrets, even made my friends and me whisper and grin as we planned our next great adventure. The spell vanished if anyone dared intrude upon our space. Privacy lasted until dinner.

Likewise, any child who played in a large cardboard box recalls its protective powers. The box became a personal castle, a private hideout, a refuge from reality where imagination could run without constraint, a sanctuary for dwelling on thoughts not of this world but for living out fantastical lives. Imaginary friends would visit to talk about things our parents could never understand.

Cardboard boxes have a distinct advantage over blanket spaces: their existence is not subject to the dinner bell. The only alteration required to transform one into a safe harbor is to cut out a window and door, each leaving a cardboard hinge. The door must be cut small and low so adults may not enter and children have to duck their heads. Once inside, they can run like rabbits through a briar patch. One sharp knife is the only tool required.

When Lori was five years old, a neighbor mentioned his new refrigerator would be delivered the following day. "Can I have the empty box?" I asked. The following morning, it sat on my front porch. Lori and Mary helped manipulate the bulky mass into our house where I proceeded to cut out windows and doors.

૭౿

A generation later, I chewed on the idea of the ultimate box house for my grandkids. If a single large refrigerator box produced so much fun, why wouldn't several boxes taped or glued together be more fun? The size, shape and configuration would be limited only by our imaginations and by finding the boxes themselves. That's it—the ultimate box house made from trash.

I didn't have space in my house to build it, but Lori and Amy both did. Made of corrugated paper, cardboard does not tolerate rain; the box house needed to be built indoors. The grandkids were old enough to help forage for boxes as well as hang out with me. I rebuffed the idea of building the house for them, like a hired carpenter, but wanted to savor their involvement in gathering boxes, identifying supplies, and designing the rooms. I especially needed them to model room dimensions and door sizes *now*. In a year the twins would be too old to play in the box house, and the youngest grandkid was now old enough to participate.

I eventually screwed up enough courage to tell Mary. "I've been thinking about building a box house out of trash at one of the girls' homes."

"Who are you building this box house for, you or the kids?"

"Probably for me, using the kids as an excuse."

"I thought so but just wanted to hear you say it."

I was the little boy Mary never had.

 ∾

Two months later, I overheard Mary on the telephone.

"Hello, Lori. You aren't going to believe this. I'm calling to let you know your daddy wants to build a box house in your home with your kids. Just wanted to warn you ahead of time. I'm going to call Amy and tell her the same thing."

Why can't I learn? My family never questions what I do as a surgeon, but when I initiate a new grandkid project, they're on the alert calling each other.

The boxes I needed were so simple and inexpensive that shopkeepers saw them as not worth saving or reusing. Supermarkets break down boxes until flat and compacted to save space. Smaller stores discard them in dumpsters.

Cocky that either of our girls would be pleased about what I was offering as a gift of time to my grandkids, I flipped a coin not wanting to show favoritism. Lori won, so I drove five blocks to see her. "Do you remember your cardboard box house with a door and a window?" I said.

"No, it had two doors and two windows," she said. "You told me you would count to three to give me time to run inside, but you never waited until three to fake a grab, and I learned never to wait 'til two. I played in it with neighborhood kids 'til it fell apart."

"You remember all that?"

"And more. You rocked the house, slapped the top—whop, then on each side—whop, whop, and mixed in, 'Fee-fi-fo-fum, I smell the blood of an Englishman.' You almost caught me, but I always ran out the back door while you grabbed at my clothes and ankles, or for extra effect, swatted me with a pillow to make me stagger and squeal as I made an exit. I ran around escaping into the other door and we would start over again. How's that for remembering?"

"Can I build a box house in your home?"

"No, I'd rather you didn't."

"Why?"

"Because you don't know when to quit."

Disappointed but not defeated, I headed for Amy whose children were younger. I practiced my sales pitch as I drove, arriving as Amy wrestled two-year-old Grant into a car seat, and blurted out my request.

"Okay," Amy said, struggling with the buckle.

"Now you understand this will be built in your roughed-out play-room and I don't know how long it will take. Probably a couple of weekends will do it. Your kids will help me and we'll bond."

"Whatever."

～

Taking a trip as a child was fun, but I derived more pleasure from a prolonged construction project, especially if several of us worked on it together. The team of my peers discussed, argued, and eventually compromised to keep the constructions moving: building a tree house from scrap wood and a model airplane from sticks. The process, not completion, became the focus. Dread hung over me when it became apparent we would finish a fun project. No embarrassing grades, no discouraging red pencil marks, no disgruntled adults.

I wanted to pass on this experience to the grandkids by teaching long-term thinking in contrast to thirty-minute television plots. Commercial toys are easily snapped together according to predetermined designs with no room for individuality. Install batteries, push buttons, and passively watch the toy function.

With grandkids involved in the process, they would take ownership and the box house would become their project. Working with me would be like helping Mom bake a cake. From a child's perspective, Mom was the bystander.

Lengthy, free-ranging conversations with the grandkids began that could compete with any boardroom strategic planning for gathering supplies, construction, and decoration. The kids crayoned great and historic structures on paper as a starting point. Startled with their knowledge, I assumed these landmarks were learned at school but soon realized the major source of information came from cartoons. Sights to be integrated into construction included the Disneyland Fantasy Castle, London Bridge, and pyramids of Egypt. Hundreds of cartoon hours trained them well. An animated version of *Lord of the Rings* became the baseline for houses built for hobbits and wizards, elves and men. Unable to compete, I contributed but a single suggestion: to use bright colors like the playhouses at McDonalds.

Gathering supplies and construction evolved into a way of life. Foraging for boxes became a test in resourcefulness and fun. Driving with me down alleys and service roads, my grandkids learned to identify the best dumpsters behind stores as opposed to entering the front door like a regular customer. They frequently advised me about large boxes behind stores or curbed as trash. They grew confident at being hoisted into a dumpster to identify and retrieve an ideal box, one with thick corrugated walls, no sign of moisture, and no staples.

I emphasized the rule of conduct around a dumpster: leave the local site as clean and orderly as we find it.

"Papa, I told my friends at school that I learned to dumpster dive for boxes," Lauren said.

"Yeah, and I told my friends how much more fun it was to dig out a good box from a dumpster than to go in the front door and spend money," Jack said.

Our assortment of boxes grew on Amy's second floor next to a walk-in attic closet. Early in the collection process, she and I tussled for space amid her Christmas decorations and broken chairs. I rationalized why my boxes and supplies were more important than decorations. After all, she would not need decorations until the Christmas season, and I would be finished in a few weekends.

Kevin, Amy's husband, joined the conversation. "I'll be glad to help you."

"Sure. We can use all of the help we can get. You understand I don't have firm plans?"

We taped some simple boxes together. Kevin soon lost interest when he realized I wanted to build another Taj Mahal. He tuned me out and turned on a basketball game.

How could we build a three-level castle using only discarded cardboard? Appliance boxes contained cardboard reinforcement corners for shipping, which rank up there with angle iron for strength. About three inches on each side of the bend, they may be as long as a refrigerator is high. A standard hacksaw proved ideal for cutting our most valuable construction component.

When the warehouse manager of Hahn TV and Appliances learned I didn't leave a mess around the dumpster and cleaned up after myself, he saw himself as an advisor for my project. "I can save some mighty strong boxes for you overnight if I know you'll pick them up the next day."

I brought photos of our progress (a grandparent usually shows photos of grandkids) to establish our credibility. He posted them on the bulletin board. Convinced it was his responsibility to supply me with the best boxes possible, he saved boxes and over one hundred corners to fill my car trunk. The estimated two-weekend project expanded to require more than a year and eight trunk-loads of corners.

A refrigerator box lying on its side could be divided into three rooms. I lined the walls, ceilings and floors with reinforced shipping corners. I experimented by placing them side-by-side to function as inner walls, ceilings and floors, like studs in a house. When each room was completed, the strength of the cardboard roof cover could compete with hardwood flooring. Adults could stand on a reinforced box. Although the walls, ceilings, and floors were not square, they worked. The kids didn't know the difference, and there wasn't a building inspector to pass judgment. With cardboard surfaces and no sharp corners, the kids would be able to career down the halls without injuries.

To hold joints together I turned to a hot glue gun. Mary had one that used four-inch pencil-sized glue sticks for hobby activities. Six of these small sticks lasted fifteen minutes of continuous gluing, but the result revealed remarkable strength, the answer for bonding. I bought an industrial glue gun at Home Depot for $5.35; local lumberyards carried ten-inch industrial-size glue sticks. One hundred big sticks lasted through three weekends of work. When, after three weeks, I returned for another hundred, the salesman asked, "What kind of work are you in?"

"Construction."

Motivated to buy the maximum for the cheapest, I purchased a case, dropping the unit price dramatically. I was now in the business of buying in volume like Walmart.

Teenagers Max and Sam wanted to help build, and I permitted them to use the glue guns. Regardless of precautions, we burned ourselves with drops of hot glue, especially me when I crawled with a headlight in confined spaces deep within a box, dragging a heated gun while the electric cord tangled my feet worse than a basket of clothes hangers. If I tried to kick the cord off, I jerked the gun back toward my face.

I strategically placed three bowls of water about the playroom for quick immersion. Despite our best intentions, we either kicked them over or they were in the wrong place when needed. Any hot glue injury was not acceptable. When the twins' doctor parents discovered their burns, Lori cornered me.

"Daddy, I saw burns on their hands at the dinner table last night. Sam said that they were only singes and Max backed him up. Want to tell me about it?"

"Uh, I picked up some latex disposable gloves. That'll take care of the singes."

"I know the difference between singes and burns. You taught me better than that. Singes don't leave marks. Let me see your hands."

I understood the implication that I was not acting responsibly. I had even been discreetly applying make-up to hide red areas on my hands before examining patients. Latex disposable gloves solved the problem, and I discarded the water bowls.

ᦇ

Reinforcement of the rooms demanded slow cutting, glue gun heating and cooling, causing me to push back estimates of stages of completion, first in weeks, then months. Amy and Kevin were satisfied that I was playing with their kids until a problem arose.

"Daddy, the kids are coming home from school wanting to work on the project and not doing their homework. Can you not be here until they've finished their homework? In fact, they have almost stopped watching TV so they can work on the box house even when you're not here."

A typical Saturday construction day began at 8:30 a.m. and, when I was on a roll, extended until 8:00 p.m. If I was working with a hot glue gun, the kids hung around and played in the rooms already built.

I took Advil for my joints like some folks take before golf, tennis or gardening, allowing me to crawl into the cramped compartments. Frequently, the work required me to sit cross-legged for an extended time deep within a box. Whether I wiggled out head first or feet first, I unfolded like an old-fashioned carpenter's rule, a slow process of leaning on the house and pushing myself up to a standing position. I took care never to grunt in the kids' presence. But, when alone and uninhibited, I grunted and groaned with gusto.

If the family was not home, audiobooks kept me company. I answered the phone so frequently that their friends and relatives grew accustomed to me and left detailed personal messages that were none of my business. If the family was home, I often let myself in without interrupting the family rhythm and left without any adult contact. Adult guests occasionally came upstairs to watch the strange gray-haired grandfather wearing a headlamp emerge from a large open-ended refrigerator box. They stood and watched for a while, then shrugged their shoulders. I could never tell whether Amy and Kevin were more proud or embarrassed of me.

Working full time and scheduling construction around my on-call responsibilities, I wanted to keep my word to the kids but reminded myself to keep the project in perspective, as my profession always came first before construction.

∽

At night I did some of my best planning, just as I had after Grandma Rosie fell asleep and I freed my imagination. After Mary fell asleep, I lay in bed staring into the darkness, planning how to add another large box, partition clever rooms, add second and third stories connected by hidden ladders and guarded by lookout towers with ramparts, and build an escape slide and trap doors.

Lori was right. What originally started as a simple box house evolved into a way of life. I didn't know when to quit.

Perhaps others saw me as strange. Perhaps others were laughing behind my back. Even I sometimes wondered if all this energy expenditure was worthwhile, and thought maybe I should be playing golf or mowing my lawn, the more traditional male activities. All doubts vanished when the grandkids came running to see what rooms or floors had been added in their absence. Yep, being considered the grandfather who was a bit different was worth it. I fell back on my mantra: "It's a matter of priorities."

The older kids began squeezing through doors. They might outgrow the box house before I finished! With the grandkids' input we partitioned, swiveled, and rotated large boxes into possible combinations. We voted and accepted the majority decision. I measured the kids to determine the height and width of doors. We intentionally kept the windows just large enough for them to see out. We stacked up three floors of boxes to the ceiling and left two open areas on top as lookout towers. Reinforced walls and ceilings ranked as high in strength as a commercial jungle gym. The kids scrambled between floors on ladders made from horizontal shipping corners between two vertical cardboard posts. The three-story house required seven ladders. An escape slide extended from the lookout tower to the second floor.

Although our original goal was to use only trash, we made two exceptions: a metal cyclone fence pole, an inch and a half in diameter. The pole functioned as a fireman's pole to escape from the third floor to the first, and I fashioned two periscopes by using two hand mirrors at 45 degrees glued together with cardboard, just like in the Boy Scout Manual. The good guys could see out over a wide area for the enemy, but the bad guys couldn't see in.

Any mystery house must have a secret room with no windows. Ours allowed, we thought, enough space for only two scrunched-up kids who entered by a spring-loaded door. A large rubber band served as the spring, but one needed to know where to find the door in the dark. When new kids were taken on a tour, our kids showed the secret room first. Soon as many as four kids crowded into this dark little space.

What is a fun house without a trap door? I stood a refrigerator box on end and built one room over the other. To enter the second floor from the first, a kid climbed a ladder and pushed up the trap door floor. With the enemy in pursuit, a kid had only to sit on the trap door. Even the smallest kids learned to use body weight to keep out the bigger ones.

One day when I drove to pick up a large box with Lauren, she asked, "Where are you going to put this room?"

"On top. This will be our last room."

"I thought we would never stop building," she said, brushing back her hair. Silent and dejected, she had come to think of our project as a way of life. So had I.

"Daddy, how's it coming?" Amy asked.

"Since I've run out of room in your playroom, we're done building. Just need to paint."

"You must be kidding me, right?"

Staring at the box house, Amy picked up the phone and dialed Kevin at work. "Break out the champagne. Daddy says he's done building."

Together, the kids and I had transformed discarded cardboard into a castle. I left paint patterns to the kids, so we returned to crayons. They drew multiple test patterns on scrap paper, and we visited the playhouse at McDonald's for ideas. Our final design painted the first floor as if it were made of brick and the top floors in bright colors. They decided chimneys, steps, and doors should be bright blue, yellow, or red.

∾

"Now tell me again why you're using oil-based paint?" Kevin asked.

"Because a water-based paint lets the lettering on the boxes bleed through and an oil-based primer won't."

"How are you going to keep paint off the floor?" Amy asked.

"With old plastic sheeting I can tape together." I laid out white sealer for the kids to brush on the entire outside structure, then stopped to admire our work of a year and a half, all accomplished without a major hitch.

I returned home and settled down to watch the evening news when our phone rang. "Daddy, you know those bright blue steps you let Grant paint? Well, he was so proud of himself, after you left he went back upstairs and stood barefoot on those pretty blue steps. You saved the carpet in the room with the drop covering, but he tracked blue steps down the stairs all the way to the kitchen. Daddy? Daddy? Daddy, are you still there?"

"Just thinking how much paint thinner I have. I can come right over and go to work."

"That's okay. You left enough thinner here for us to work with. Between me, Kevin, and Lauren, we pretty well got it all. Took some of the varnish off several stair steps. Looks a little different, but we'll get used to it. Daddy, can you find something else to do next weekend and let my family rest? This will give the kids a chance to catch up on their homework. Maybe take Mom to a movie."

Two weeks later, we used a yardstick to draw parallel pencil lines over the white background painted around the first floor of the house. We dipped the side of a brick-sized kitchen sponge into a tray of bright red paint. When pressed onto the white background, it looked like pitted brick with three-eighths inch spacing for white mortar. Then bright colors on the second and third floors. The final effect was excellent, if I do say so myself.

"What do you think, kids?"

Lauren grinned at me. "Papa, it's the most beautiful castle in the world. I'll never do anything else like this in my whole life. Since our last name is King, we'll name it the King Castle."

"I love you," Keegan said.

The interior walls, floors, and ceilings continued to undergo modifications without my presence. The kids used crayons and notes from school for decoration.

❧

As far as the kids are concerned, they were involved at every stage of construction and were the prime builders; I only assisted. They perceived my role as the driver who picked up boxes. The box house smelled of protection and love. The small dim rooms provided a sanctuary from adults where the kids could engage their fantasies of slaying dragons, hiding from the bad guy, or just coloring the walls. Sometimes they simply hid from the world there, dreamed, and acted as if they couldn't hear Mom calling the first three times.

The house built from discarded boxes showed minimal wear after one year of use which surprised everyone except me and the kids. The wear power became obvious after being the center of attention for four or five kids, and, on occasion, more than twenty.

The final product was too heavy to move and eventually would need to be demolished once the kids physically outgrew the doors and rooms. Only a chainsaw would penetrate the reinforcements throughout the walls and floors. Like ignoring the inevitable death of a parent, we never brought up dismantling our creation.

After the second year, we learned that cardboard hinges of the doors break down first, and a ladder between floors showed loose rungs easy to patch. I was pleased to see the evidence of thousands of hours of play.

☙

Once upon a time, my sanctuary had been a blanket over kitchen chairs. A generation later, I chased my daughters through a cardboard box with two doors and two windows. Another generation and I chased my grandkids through the ultimate box house. They ducked and scrunched up their shoulders and scrambled into their lair. Generations braided together as I chased them into hiding places, slapped the sides—whop, whop—and said, "Fe-fi-fo-fum, I smell the blood of an Englishman," while my hand extended blindly into a room, searching for little ones.

We experienced patience, persistence, and the strength of bonding for a common purpose. Also, we found that eighteen months is not long when we are having good family time. My child within earned one more niche in my transformation, and my heart was full. Mary was right. The box house was mostly for me, another step in fulfilling my goal of redemption to offset my remorse about not being available when needed. My time was well spent.

How far will the roots of my efforts reach? How can I know or even dream what those seeds will bear? Yet another generation may need to pass before someone tastes the fruit.

Back: Keegan, Lauren; Front: Grant, Jack

The Box House aka The King Kastle

Box House Stats

1	Balcony
1	Trapdoor
1	Escape slide
1	Secret room
1	Fireman's escape pole, from top to bottom
2	Lookout towers
2	Pillboxes, for kids to raise their heads against the box ceiling and see out
2	Periscopes
3	Floors, each as high as a kitchen table
5	Tools: hacksaw, box knife, craft glue gun, yardstick, headlamp
7	Internal ladders
7	Industrial glue guns (six wore out)
17	Rooms
240	Dollars spent, mostly for glue sticks, zero for scavenged boxes and excess paint
300	Square feet, equaling an efficiency apartment, bigger than the two-room house my family of five moved into after returning from California
565	Days of construction (one year, six months, two weeks, three days)
2,000	Ten-inch glue sticks
0	Real estate value
∞	Heart value

Domino Fever

Clickety-clickety-clack . . .

As a kid, I developed a passion to play with dominoes. Not for the game but for themselves. Whenever upright dominoes began their fall, I mimicked their clacking sound by holding my breath and clicking my tongue with them as if I were singing along with a favorite tune on the radio. Their sound was always mesmerizing.

After stacking dominoes, standing them upright and sideways, and using them to build forts, bridges, and castles, I began creating more inventive falls. Sometimes a line of dominoes would fall up and over books, around doors, under the bed and out the other side, my imagination limited solely by the number of dominoes available.

I borrowed dominoes from neighborhood kids and adults under false pretenses: my parents were having a party and needed more sets, or my grandparents were coming to visit and the stores were closed on Sundays. Careful to mark the sets with crayons to distinguish ownership before using them in my elaborate designs, I easily wiped them clean before returning them. Sometimes my stash included five borrowed sets at one time: one hundred sixty-seven dominoes in a single fall because an elderly neighbor had a set of double-twelves.

❦

The Stewart grandkids owned a cache of thirty toy cardboard building blocks decorated as large bricks that could be stood up and tripped to fall like dominoes. If only I had more, many more, to help them create an elaborate fall. Close in size and shape to Kleenex boxes, a string of blocks and boxes would be more dramatic than small dominoes, especially if they could be integrated with common items found around the house.

Keegan's sixth birthday was coming up in three weeks. That's it! His celebration could be used to show him how to make dominoes fall in a creative way—my gift to him. My agenda, of course, was to use his birthday as an excuse to produce an over-the-top production and pass it off as education. I could round up his siblings and cousins as a team to recapture my own childhood fun.

I stopped by the King house. With Keegan holding my hand, my plan unfolded. "For Keegan's birthday, I would like to set up a string of upright boxes to fall like dominoes. Right here in your kitchen could be one of the places."

Amy narrowed her eyes. "What do you mean by *one of the places?*"

"The kids will start a ball rolling from upstairs that drops off the balcony to the kitchen, then runs through the living room, down the hall, up the stairs, into the bedrooms and down the backstairs."

Kevin shook his head and grinned. "How do you make boxes fall up the stairs?"

"If we tape one box on top of another, the two will be tall enough to reach the step above."

Amy raised her eyebrow. "How long have you been thinking about this?"

I studied the top of Keegan's head. "About thirty years. I know where to get enough boxes. If we start right after school on a Friday, we can be finished the next day. It'll be easy. No damage will be done and we'll clean up everything."

Amy and Kevin found the proposition awkward to reject with Keegan standing next to me, his eyes focused on theirs. What could a parent do?

"I'll meet with all the grandkids to block off their time and give them the lowdown," I said. The potential bonanza of boxes had yet to be confirmed.

Before my plan crystalized, the phone rang and rang with calls from the grandkids.

"Papa, I think we should build this line going out the back door, around the house and into the front door," eight-year-old Lauren said.

"If I could have the bathroom and fill the tub, I can make my boxes fall the length of the tub without getting wet," thirteen-year-old Sam said.

"I could shoot the first one with a BB gun to start the fall," eight-year-old Jack said.

"Since it's Keegan's sixth birthday, I could place a candle on six boxes and light them. When they fall it will knock out the flame," thirteen-year-old Max said.

Oops! They were going to need safety guidelines.

∾

The next week I bought a case of forty-eight Kleenex boxes at Office Depot. Keegan's birthday was two weeks away, and I needed to prove to myself that the boxes would stand and fall as imagined. When the fun was over, we would divvy up the Kleenex among the King, Stewart, and Battenfield families.

My car trunk hid the case until Mary left for a dental appointment. I brought the boxes inside and stood them on end, trying different spacing until settling on the optimum space with the best angles to turn a corner. My plan was going to work.

Back at the King house to celebrate Grant's third birthday, I surreptitiously stepped off my proposed track. With the twists and turns I imagined, the distance came to one hundred thirty feet. My plan called for a box about every six inches, requiring 260 boxes.

∾

Monday I located the employee who stocked my office daily with paper products and asked to borrow Kleenex boxes.

"Borrow? How do you return Kleenex?" she said. "That's like returnin' toilet paper."

"The boxes won't be opened."

"If you're not gonna open 'em, what're you gonna do with 'em?"

"Stand them on end and let them fall like dominoes. Six grandkids will be building with me."

"Build? That'll crush my boxes."

"Not stack the boxes. We'll stand them up and let them fall in a line."

"Like dominoes?"

"Yeah. We won't damage a single box. I'd like to pick up four cases on Wednesday and return them early Monday morning."

Tuesday I made each grandkid responsible for one zone of falling boxes integrated with items from around the house. One kid's fall line had to begin at the door, circle the room, and exit in alignment with the next kid's boxes. While I was making plans for an extravaganza behind the backs of Amy and Kevin, they had yet to give me clearance to invade their house for the weekend. By now it was too awkward for them to refuse in front of their children, especially the birthday boy.

Wednesday I loaded my car with the Stewarts' cardboard building blocks, my personal case of Kleenex, and four borrowed cases from the office.

Thursday the kids helped me unload my car, distributing 270 blocks and boxes throughout the Kings' home, along hallways, up and down the stairs, in every room but the bathrooms and off-limits master bedroom. Our fall line would measure over 200 linear feet.

Friday after school six grandkids scrambled for items from the utility closet, kitchen, and garage.

"No paint cans, nothing toxic. Nothing that can spill. Stay away from big tools, and use your imagination."

They spread items onto the kitchen floor for display: ice cream scoop, graduating bowls, soup ladles, canned goods, plastic cups, marbles, box-end wrenches, duct tape, toilet plunger, a vacuum cleaner hose, books, magazines, toothpicks, golf balls, a funnel.

As they designed their fall lines, the kids could return to the kitchen and choose what worked for them.

With all six grandkids present, I stood ten boxes on end and demonstrated how far apart to place them and how to turn a corner by tripping the first box. "Now you stand up ten boxes and practice." Even three-year-old Grant followed the instructions to success. "Okay, now make your plans crazy. Experiment with your assigned zone by adding household items. A simple line of falling boxes is not enough. Don't be concerned if you can't think of how to incorporate an item. Once you start, ideas will pop into your head. Anyone can line up boxes and make them fall and not one of you is *anyone.* Think ahead: your fall line must end with a flair. Your assigned section must line up with the one before and following you." I needed to be the general referee as well as assure that one zone of boxes aligned with the next.

We worked until Amy had dinner ready, gulped our food, and continued on. Each kid started with a simple fall line but curiosity drove them all to peek at each other's progress. Ideas expanded; kids elaborated. Competing like they were killing snakes, their pace picked up and creativity increased. Before their fall line could cross their zone, a bigger and better idea crowded out the original simple plan.

Innovative juices flooded their minds as they ran to the kitchen floor to choose household items. Canned goods became a common choice to build bridges over falling boxes. If one kid built a bridge from canned goods, another built one bigger and more elaborate. By 10:00 p.m. I forced the Stewart boys to shut down and ride home with me so the King kids could go to bed.

Saturday morning at 9:30 a.m. construction began again. We discovered a recurring problem. When someone bumped a box, a long row began falling and continued into adjoining zones, resulting in yells and accusations. The kids, more agile than me, seldom tripped a box. "Papa, if you'll pick up your feet a little higher, you won't bump my boxes," Keegan said.

I wandered down the hall into Jack's zone. "If you'll just stand by the door, Papa, you can see everything. Lauren may need some help. You might check on her."

We solved the problem by laying down every eighth box to limit an accidental fall to seven between the new "safety boxes." Another problem arose. Double-high piggy-backs reached the next step but proved to be inherently unstable. They required the fiddle factor; Max jockeyed broken toothpicks as shims to achieve balance.

Standing two wastebaskets on end, Max bridged them with a pipe wrench and tied a soup ladle to hang below. He pulled the ladle back in the up position to rest precariously on a Kleenex box. When this was struck, the ladle swung forward striking the next box. The swinging ladle worked so well he added two more ladles, making three swings in a row.

Arguments abounded, especially when one kid's creativity did not align with the fall line in the adjoining zone. The drama of final alignment simulated the joining of the first transcontinental railroad from opposite directions at Promontory Summit, Utah.

Alongside the string of boxes in the hall, I stood a row of actual dominoes to be bumped by one of the falling Kleenex boxes. This spur line would fall for three feet without fanfare or inclusion of household items.

"Papa, what are the dominoes for?" Sam asked.

"For me and old times' sake."

All afternoon the kids improved their zones and guarded them as if they were military posts. By then everyone understood there was absolutely no trespassing into anyone else's zone. Lauren positioned chairs with a bed sheet to conceal her creation. The kids continued tweaking their fall lines into ever more complex designs.

Amy and Kevin caught Domino Fever and joined me in policing and arbitration.

We were now one day behind our estimated hour of completion. Delay after delay pushed the Great Fall to Sunday. Grandkids' expectations surpassed my expectations, a welcome tonic for any grandfather.

∽

Sunday afternoon at 4:30 p.m. I spoke with a voice of authority through a bullhorn. "Revisions will now cease! IT'S SHOWTIME! Please man your posts. On the count of five, all of you but Keegan will stand up the safety boxes in your zones. On the count of ten, Keegan will start his engine. According to our agreed-upon plan, you will stay where you are to make sure the boxes remain standing and all goes well. When the Great Fall has passed through your zone, it's okay to follow. Got that? Ten, nine, eight, seven, six, five … "

The plan immediately fell apart. No one, including the kids, anticipated their excitement. Two days of competition, concentration, and construction created a frenzied crowd. One yelled and the others started screaming. They abandoned their zones, stumbled over each other, and ran to the starting point, never once tripping a falling box.

"Stay right where you are, Papa," Jack said, running past.

Having watched Keegan practice the opening move of the show, the kids now wanted to see the real event. Me, too. We crowded into his zone as he operated a remote-controlled car that rolled mysteriously from beneath his bed, picked up speed, drove down the hall into a recreation room, and climbed a leaning ironing board to the top of a table. Keegan ran behind his car and everyone followed him.

"Papa, stand still," Lauren scolded as she ran past.

A three-foot tube from Christmas wrapping paper sloped down the edge of the table at twenty degrees. A golf ball resting against a toothpick stub lay in wait, balanced in the mouth of the tube. The remote-controlled car gently bumped the ball, which rolled down inside the tube, emptying into three feet of coiled vacuum cleaner hose. We followed the sound of the ball spiraling, turning, and emptying onto an old couch elevated ten inches on books at one end. The ball rolled down the middle of twelve books laid open like sloping shingles, dropped between two balusters of the balcony over the edge down to the kitchen table on the first floor where Sam had placed Kleenex boxes in a T-shape. When the transverse box received the falling golf ball on one end, it flipped like a teeter-totter, striking a new row of boxes.

A marble resting on one of the now-falling boxes began rolling across the kitchen table, slightly uneven due to a *Reader's Digest* under each leg at one end. The marble rolled through a one-inch alley between book spines and dropped into a funnel duct-taped between the seats of two chairs. The funnel spout was perfectly aimed to drop the marble on the inside rim of the first of three graduated mixing bowls spaced six inches apart. It gained momentum as it rolled down the inside wall and shot up the opposite side of each bowl, arced through the air, and dropped into the next smaller bowl. Pong! Pang! Ping! The marble was now a missile leaving Sam's creation and heading toward a vulnerable box of Kleenex.

Yelling and scrambling down the stairs, we all tried to catch up with the already falling boxes on the first floor. The fall made soft thuds as it curved in a circle around an easy chair and climbed a three-inch staircase of *Reader's Digests* so when the line arrived at boxes already down, it reached over and struck an upright box on the other side, completing a perfect circle.

The line passed under a table. Emerging on the other side, it split around a chair into two rows simultaneously rejoining with perfect timing on both sides. Again, the line split around a second chair with perfect joining past the chair.

"Hallelujah!" we hollered as though we had landed a man on the moon.

A tumbling Kleenex box bumped my first domino causing the rest to fall *clickety-clickety-clack*, the mesmerizing sound from my childhood.

After the cascade passed through the living and dining rooms, it reached the foot of the front stairs. "Climb, climb, climb," Max yelled as the piggy-backs worked their way up the stairs. The rest of us joined in as though the boxes could hear: "Climb! Climb! Climb!"

Once the fall reached the top of the stairs, it returned to single boxes and continued down the hall into Lauren's room. Max had helped her move a three-foot oval vanity mirror from her bedroom corner to the center of the floor. He released the friction knob enabling it to lie level with the floor and rotate freely. A book balanced on a box provided the weight to fall on one end and spin the mirror. On the opposite end of the mirror Lauren had taped a plastic spoon with the cup of the spoon extending past the edge. The book fell, the mirror spun, and the spoon tipped over another line of boxes continuing out the door and down the hall.

The running, cheering, and screaming escalated. We were Keystone Cops stumbling down a narrow alley as we tried to keep up with the falling boxes while staying out of the way. Kids ran along each side of the tumbling boxes, anxious to see how their own zone performed.

Everyone in the house was infected with Domino Fever. Kevin tried to video the event but couldn't look through a viewfinder while running and stepping over kids and fallen boxes.

I hollered to Mary waiting at the bottom of the backstairs, "LOAD. GRANT. NOW." Mary lifted three-year-old Grant onto the seat of a twelve-inch-wide Playskool plastic car resting on a toy roller coaster running fifteen feet down into the hall. Broken matchsticks shimmed under the rear wheels held the car, ready and waiting for a slight bump.

In the meantime, boxes cascaded down the backstairs while the family chased and screamed. Three boxes above Grant supported progressively-sized box-end wrenches. Grinning, Grant sat in the car looking back over his shoulder at boxes falling down the stairs.

The last, and heaviest, wrench thumped the rear of the car. It coasted halfway down the hall toward a roll of butcher paper stretched between two cartons of Coke. Jack had taped a wooden cooking spoon on the front of the car as a battering ram. The ram bumped the roll that fell and unfurled down the hall, reading "Happy Birthday, Keegan" in large print. It then struck a clothespin attached to the "on" button of a boom box. The house exploded with a loud "Who Let the Dogs Out" followed by "Happy Birthday to You."

"Do it again, Papa!" the kids yelled. "Let's do it again!"

Impossible. Neither Keegan nor I would ever be six again.

A Single Leg of Kleenex Boxes Splitting and
Rejoining Past a Chair

Trapeze

In 2003, the biggest toy I ever saw dominated a small park along the west bank of the Arkansas River near the 21st Street Bridge. A spider web of tension-adjusted locking cables tapering down to metal stakes driven into the ground supported the superstructure. Six aluminum struts as large as telephone poles soared skyward in dramatic contrast to the grassy field and surrounding trees. The rig's dizzying height and breadth created shards of blue sky. A massive safety net with curved ends stretched six feet off the ground beneath it. Two high trapeze bars hung in stillness.

As a nineteen-year-old in 1956, I daydreamed about flying through the air after watching the movie *Trapeze*. Burt Lancaster played a seasoned trapeze artist who understood the value of an outstanding act that sold tickets. His character fell without a net while attempting a record-breaking triple somersault. Despite the resulting ankle injury that caused a permanent limp, he learned to be a catcher. Developing the reputation in trapeze circles as the best catcher in the business, he became consumed with catching the first flyer in history to complete the triple somersault.

Tony Curtis, a flyer new to the circus, displayed the most potential to fulfill Lancaster's dream and became his student. Recognized as the star of the show, Curtis hopped off a high platform holding the primary trapeze bar and took the first of three swings to build momentum: forward, back, forward. He released at the top of the second forward swing to perform his best trick. Lancaster snatched him out of the air as easily as if he were netting a butterfly. Orchestral music enhanced the epic drama. Gina Lollobrigida, a beautiful Italian starlet in a tight, revealing leotard, completed the romantic triangle.

Scenes of humans flying through the air mesmerized me when they defied gravity and were caught wrist-to-wrist in midair by another trapeze artist before falling gracefully into the net. Simmering hormones made me vulnerable to the convergence of music, movies, adventure, romance, and girls. I envied the men's trapeze skills and lusted for Gina. My fascination with the art of the trapeze never diminished through succeeding decades.

∽

Twenty years later, when the Ringling Bros. and Barnum & Bailey Circus came to Tulsa, a trapeze artist injured his shoulder during a performance and was referred to my orthopedic practice. While we waited for his x-rays to develop, his solemn presence impressed me. So did the fact that he physically resembled Tony Curtis in 1956. After confirming his x-rays showed no dislocations or fractures, I examined his shoulder and explained his injury was a strain that would clear in a few days. Busting a gut to talk about the movie, I tried to look casual. "Have you ever seen the movie *Trapeze*?" He nodded.

"What did you think about Tony Curtis throwing a triple somersault?"

"That was me. I doubled for him. Most people don't remember the movie, much less me."

"Well, I do! Let me shake your hand. Can I have your autograph?"

He grinned as he wrote "Fay Alexander" across the front of his chart. Though not the first to throw a triple somersault, he was one of the early artists to push the limits of the physically demanding circus act created in 1859 by Louis Léotard, a Frenchman who first performed aerial tumbling tricks over a swimming pool wearing the costume he himself stitched for dramatic effect.

∽

Back to 2003.

I was sixty-six years old when a troupe of enterprising young trapeze artists pooled their talent, money, and credit to establish the

Evolution Flying Trapeze School in Tulsa. The Tulsa Parks Department granted them permission to assemble the trapeze on the west side of the river. Shortly after the school opened for business, I stood slack-jawed in the park watching two daring young men taking turns on a flying trapeze. A third narrated the flyer's moves to an audience of five.

Every day after work, drawn to the trapeze like a moth to flame, I stopped to gawk at classes of new students. First the enthusiastic troupe gave a fifteen-minute exhibition beginning with simple swings off the platform. Then they flew and caught each other in mid-air demonstrating leg catches, pirouettes, and layouts. Occasionally working without a catcher, a flyer hurled himself higher than the frame of the rig and fell gracefully through the air with a full twist, double somersault or swan dive into the net. I was right up there with him. They needed students.

Josh, the first one to greet newcomers by stepping forward with his hand out for a shake, was the charmer of the troupe with his flashing smile. In town less than twenty-four hours, he secured a date with a girl from the camera crew of a local television station.

Eli, the biggest and most muscular of the trapeze artists, was the obvious catcher, although all three were talented enough to rotate roles. The catcher's job was to hang upside down by his knees from the secondary bar and swing by pumping his head, arms, and body. When satisfied with the height of his swing, he called out "Hep!" The stern, unmistakable code word commanded the flyer holding the primary bar to hop off the platform without hesitation *now*.

Anton revealed himself as the leader by the way Josh and Eli deferred questions to him. Although Anton talked less, his eye contact and body carriage set him apart. Even climbing the ladder to the platform, he did so with grace and confidence. On the platform, he lifted his chin in a pose a little higher than the others and nodded his head to the audience with a smile, as though saying, *You ain't seen nothin' yet.*

Standing at attention to wait for the catcher's cue, Anton gazed straight ahead, never looking at the audience again, his stance and slow purposeful movements commanding our attention. Grabbing the bar, he hopped off the platform and whipped his body like a massive, wet rope while gaining speed and height. The top of his returning swing found him four feet higher than the platform. He arrived at the peak of his next forward swing a split second ahead of the catcher, giving himself time to release and hurl even higher. He pulled his knees into a tucked position and rotated through a masterful double somersault. For two seconds, he broke free of earth's bonds and grabbed an experience few will ever dare to own—release from gravity. But gravity won and he fell, opening from his tuck into a full layout position with arms outstretched. He didn't just hope Eli would be there—*he knew*. With perfect timing, Eli reached the apex of his swing and stalled with his hands out waiting for Anton. Wrists locked together, they continued swinging down and up as one. Eli still had momentum when he pitched Anton away. In unison they swan dived into the net. Ballet in the air.

Flies could have swarmed in my mouth. Afraid to get too close, fearing I might accept their invitation to join a class, I watched exhibitions for the next two weeks from the parking lot instead of sitting on one of the twenty-one folding chairs provided for an audience.

One afternoon Anton brought along a young lady. In short order it became obvious they had trapeze experience together. Her petite frame didn't walk as much as it flowed. Leaving the platform with a dainty hop, she generated more height with each swing and released the bar in a full layout somersault with her head back and chest out, rotating through the air while gaining altitude. As she fell, Anton appeared at the perfect moment as the catcher, swinging as he locked her wrists. They bottomed out on the arc and began the upswing. Reaching maximum height when her weight was nil, he pulled her arms up and kissed her, holding the kiss through the entire backswing, then released her to the net. The combination of flying and kissing buckled my knees. My heady mind supplied the romantic French café music.

All three members of the troupe were needed to hold class, of any size: the catcher hanging from the secondary bar, the instructor standing on the platform, and the safety-line handler standing on the ground. The line handler applied a well-padded safety belt to the student's waist before he or she climbed the ladder. The instructor helped the student across the gap to the platform and snapped safety lines to the padded belt. From this point forward, the student could not fall. He or she would be released slowly into the net after a swing.

On a Friday evening I called a grandson. "Max, I want you to come with me in the morning to see something. You might be interested. Ask your mother if it's okay to visit a trapeze demonstration. Lauren is coming, too."

✎

My grandkids knew what we did together was usually fun so they went along with my ideas. Did I have an agenda? Yes. The trapeze represented a step for my family to continue welcoming new experiences. Beneath the surface of the invitation lurked my second agenda: watching my grandkids take lessons might give me the nerve to join a class.

The following morning, I picked up fourteen-year-old Max and ten-year old Lauren and drove to watch a lesson. The three of us sat in the back row of the folding chairs through two thirty-minute classes, listening and watching the audience of friends and families cheer and clap.

"I'll go if you will," Max said as a challenge to Lauren.

Lauren smiled. "Okay, if you go first," she said, surprising us both.

The kids listened closely to the orientation in a class of four. First up, Max was outfitted with the safety belt and climbed the ladder. Anton helped him onto the platform, snapped the safety lines to his belt, and showed him how to hold the trapeze bar. He coached Max about critical timing when hopping off the platform. Max hopped and swung forward. At the top of his swing, he scrambled his knees over the bar, swung back, and released his hands. As he swung forward again, hanging by his knees, arms outstretched and head extended, he looked for the catcher. On the third try, his timing improved enough to be caught. Lauren followed and, after several misses, completed a catch.

Pacing like a coach on the sidelines, I hollered and cheered them on with each catch or miss. On the way home they chattered on an emotional high, anxious to tell their parents. They wanted to return to learn more complex moves like straddling the bar and flying off the top of the bar.

Surprised they took a lesson on our first visit, it was now time for me to make a decision. During thirty-minute lunch breaks, I gulped what would go down fast, drove five minutes to the trapeze, watched a class, and returned to work. A regular observer, I lingered at the edge of the grass like a hungry stray dog wanting to come forth but held back by the unknown. Although I tried to be discreet, the friendly troupe recognized me and often smiled and waved. One day a lone folding chair sat where I usually stood.

Nights after visiting the trapeze, I drifted into sleep rehearsing a triple somersault with vivid sensations of soaring, spinning, and falling. Days I mentally rehearsed the basic swing like a basketball player rehearses sinking a shot.

☙

One day at the park, checking to make sure there were no spectators, I screwed up my courage and strolled across a wide patch of grass toward Anton, my potential teacher.

"Do you have an upper age limit?"

"No. You're never too old to learn or have fun."

He shook my hand and formally introduced himself, reassuring me I was a good candidate if only because I had watched my grandkids succeed. The more we visited, I learned he carried a distinguished background in dancing, diving, floor gymnastics, and circus trapeze. As students began arriving, he asked about my goals with my grandkids, as well as my own.

"Have you ever seen the movie *Trapeze*?" I blurted out.

"Sure. Have it on DVD. A real classic. Made before I was born."

I winced and excused myself to watch a new class. If ever my fantasy were to be fulfilled, I needed to act soon or forever be remembered as the guy who always stood in the background. Until one day he didn't show.

The following Saturday, before the nine o'clock students filtered into the park, I paused alone in my car long enough to watch the troupe prepare the trapeze and, in particular, secure the net, as it and the ladder were always kept in nearby storage overnight. Wearing tennis shoes, loose-fitting workout pants, and a tee shirt, I killed the engine and got out. Squaring my shoulders, I pulled out my shirttail, ruffled my hair, and marched toward the rig, right up to Anton. "I want to sign up for a lesson!"

"We've been expecting you. You've been practicing in your head over there by yourself."

By the time I finished signing release forms and paying fifteen dollars, Josh had assumed his position on the platform with Anton as the line handler below. No catcher was necessary for my climb up the ladder, a nervous transfer to the platform, and a swing or two.

Anton attached the safety belt around my waist. Viewed from the base of the ladder, the platform disappeared into the clouds. My heart rate increased with each step. Grandkids did this! The first twenty steps of the climb stretched out in agonizing slow motion. At least I'm an orthopedic surgeon and know how to fix broken bones. The next dozen steps were heart-stopping. What was I thinking? I paused at the top before stepping across the void. Josh took my hand to help me onto the platform, providing reassurance as he had to hundreds of students. "Let's stand here while you get your bearings."

My hands grabbed the platform's support cables in a death grip. I looked down, imagining a fall. The long, wide net was deep enough to keep me from bouncing out. From my perch three stories high, I looked over treetops up the Arkansas River until it turned west and down the river to Zinc Dam. Miniature joggers moved along River Parks Trail. Downtown Tulsa from the Williams Building to the Phil-tower was mine.

Josh snapped the safety lines onto my belt, powdered my hands with chalk, pulled the trapeze bar over with a long pole, and held it steady for me. My knuckles turned white up to my elbows. Someone would have to shoot me before I would release that bar.

"I can't swing with you. You'll do it by yourself, okay?"

"Okay," I whispered.

"Remember, no catches this time. When I count to three, you will take a small hop off the platform and swing forward, back, forward, before you let go. If you get tired, let go. Anton will lower you into the net." *If only he would put a hand on my shoulder and say I'm going to do fine.*

I sucked in a deep breath and hopped off into space. After three swings, I released the bar and was lowered into the net. Anton coached me to crawl across the net, grasp the edge, hang my head over, and roll off into a standing position. He released the lines from my safety belt, clipped them together, and sent them back up to Josh. Standing tall on the ground, I took my second deep breath since climbing the ladder and looked around for the cheering audience. A lone jogger ran in place while he watched, shook his head, checked his time, and continued down the trail.

Waiting on the platform for me with a big smile, Josh patted me on the back and punched the air with his right hand in congratulation. "You're going to make a catch this time. Remember, three swings. Forward, back, forward. Before your third swing, you need to be hanging from the bar by your knees so your hands will be free to reach out and locks wrists with Eli at the top of his swing. When you hear him say 'Gotcha,' straighten your legs so they slip off the bar. Anton has you by the safety lines. You can't fall. Eli is beginning his swing. When he hollers, 'Hep,' you hop off *now*."

Eli swung from the secondary bar, increasing his height with the same fluid action used on a playground swing. When he reached his maximum height, he slipped backwards from sitting to hanging upside down by his knees, freeing his hands to catch me.

"Hep!"

I hopped.

To be successful, we had to coordinate our maximum height at our closest point—together. If I were one second late, he would be out of the catch zone. At the top of my first forward swing, I quickly threw my knees over the bar. At the top of the return swing, I released my hands and hung only by my knees, swinging forward with my hands hanging free in empty space, reaching for Eli. The trapeze required faith. The thrill of flying through the air exceeded my fear. I never saw him coming.

"Gotcha!" Eli blurted as we locked wrists at the peak of our swings. My knees automatically straightened to release the bar. We now swung outside time as one. I forgot to breathe. I wanted to grab the moment by the collar and scream, "Don't let this end." He released me to Anton who lowered me into the net. I crawled off, heart racing, grinning. Anton unclipped the safety lines. Running to the ladder to fly through the air again helped release a build-up of tension in the cheeks of my butt. I wished the joyous day could last forever.

When I told Mary about my lesson on the trapeze, her eyes rolled in the way only she could do. I didn't tell anyone else, afraid someone would throw a net over me. Mary, however, understood my enthusiasm as normal. The next afternoon, she talked to Lori and Amy on the speakerphone. "Your daddy took a trapeze lesson on Saturday morning. Thought I should tell you just so you won't be surprised when he asks you to go along. Down by Riverside Park on the west side. Well, what do you two think?"

"No obligation for us to take a lesson, okay? See you there Saturday morning. We'll just watch. Thanks for the tip, Mom."

༄

Within the next two weeks, Lori, Amy, and the other grandkids took lessons. After four-year-old Grant watched his family on the trapeze, he did not want to be left out. Too short to hang by his knees and cover the distance needed to reach for a catch, he hung by his hands and was long enough for Eli to grab him by the ankles. When Grant let go of the bar, he completed his swing with Eli. Although upside down, his swing qualified as a catch. No one in my family ever crawled off the net without a flushed face and big grin.

Friends and relatives joined us. We even celebrated a birthday with a trapeze party. Three grandkids were invited to be part of a public trapeze exhibition, an experience they later used on their résumés. I took lessons with the patient troupe through two May-October seasons and was, by far, the oldest student to learn how to perform a full-release back somersault and make a catch. After fifty or so misses, that is.

The Evolution Flying Trapeze School closed due to a lack of students. I occasionally still drive to the edge of the park. Well-groomed grass covers the small area where the trapeze once stood and fulfilled my dream. I gather comfort knowing we all mastered our fear and seized a day which may never come our way again. Alone in my car, I feel myself hop off the platform, swing forward, back, forward, release and somersault through the air, knowing I will be caught. The crowd roars. Tony Curtis never had it so good.

The Catcher and Max

Harold's Death Grip

New Year's Eve

I favor traditions.

When Max and Sam were five years old, they spent New Year's Eve with us while Lori and Doug attended a party. Mary and I brainstormed an evening of entertainment in case the boys stayed awake until midnight. What began as a one-night babysitting event grew into an annual tradition as two grandkids increased to six. When Grant was three, old enough to join in as a player for the festivities, Mary and I approached Lori and Amy. "We would like permission to allow your kids to eat candy for dinner," I said.

Questioned, I fumbled for a mature explanation. After all, these were daughters standing before us whom we taught to limit sweets, brush their teeth, and eat broccoli.

"On New Year's Eve, I want to take them to the supermarket," I said, "give them four dollars each and have them buy candy for their dinner. They have to stay within their dollar limit, can't trade or give away candy, and will learn to get the most for their money. The older ones can help the little ones stay within a budget."

"What are you and Mom up to now?"

"We expect them to be up late," Mary said, "so we'll rent movies to start after midnight for those who can stay awake. They'll bring sleeping bags and sleep on the floor in front of the TV. Harold and I will go to bed."

"We'll make them brush their teeth," I said, throwing in the idea as a negotiating tool.

❧

With Christmas two days past and New Year's Eve three days ahead, I drove by a Christmas tree lot at 41st and Harvard scattered with remnants of unsold and broken trees. The lot looked like the morning after. I studied a homemade contraption next to a portable storage shed. Two weeks earlier I had spied the metal hoop mounted on a plywood table the size of a Ping Pong table and pondered possibilities. For hauling purposes, one pushed a Christmas tree stump first through the hoop while netting pressed down the limbs without breaking them: no motor, no gears, no moving parts.

I greeted the owner, trying to charm him with a smile as a prelude to my request.

Assuming I wanted a tree, he said, "You're about two days late, but I can make you a great bargain."

"I'm looking at that netting you put around Christmas trees. I want to run my grandkids through the hoop and stretch netting over them."

"Are we on *Candid Camera?*" he said, lifting one of his woolen ear flaps.

"No, you're safe. I always try to do something silly with my grandkids on New Year's Eve. I'll leave their heads out one end of the netting, cut holes for their arms and have their legs out the bottom far enough so they can hobble. They'll be going to the supermarket like this. They're expecting something, they just don't know what."

"I'll be here with a truck," he said, "to haul off this stuff on New Year's Eve. Bring them by before 5:00 p.m., and I'll slide them across the table through the net. This will use up the rest of the netting, and I won't have to store it for a year. Besides, I want to see this."

҂

I called the grandkids. "Here's the plan for this year. I'll pick you up at 4:30, but before we go shopping for your dinner, I'll take you on a quick errand. You gotta be good sports and follow what I say."

When we pulled up to the desolate tree lot, the kids' jabbering stopped. I turned off the engine and sat in silence, milking my captive audience before springing the plan.

"Papa, there's nothing here," Lauren said. "This place is empty."

"Not so. You need costumes to buy your dinner, and we're going to find them here."

They piled out of the car in anticipation without knowing about what. Almost as excited as the kids, the owner waved them forward. "Follow me." Six grandkids gathered wide-eyed around the plywood table. "We lay a Christmas tree on the table and push it through that hoop. The netting drags over the tree and keeps down the branches. We're going to do the same with you. Who's first?" Max climbed onto the table while the others stood open-mouthed. "Lie on your back with your arms crossed, son. Keep your knees stiff and we'll push you through by your feet. One of you other kids help push his feet." The net cocooned Max head to foot. The owner took a photograph. "I gotta prove this."

We helped Max off the table into an upright position and before I could cut holes for his arm and the bottom of the net at his knee level, the others scrambled for their turns. Lauren lined up for the hoop with her arms across her chest. In quick succession we bagged them all. They hit the ground like bird dogs jumping out of the back of a truck after a long ride. They soon discovered that with an easy hip or shoulder bump, they could tip over their siblings and cousins. Before I could thank the owner, they developed teams and strategies to bump others off balance, careening around like wobbly bowling pins vulnerable to the slightest touch. Their speech shifted from normal babble to goofy talk.

If the police had seen us at that moment, they would have netted me. I didn't dare consider what Mary might do.

ᖇ

All the way to the supermarket, I worried about the kids surprising the clerks. What if employees interpreted this as a group prank to distract and shoplift or even rob the store? The closer we got, the more I fretted.

Parked close outside the store, I turned to the kids. "It's okay to take off your seatbelts, but wait here. Give me about five minutes, then come on in wearing your nets."

I approached the nearest clerk. "Some kids will be coming in here to buy candy," I said with a glib smile. "They'll be wearing strange costumes, and I don't want anyone to be surprised. They're good, polite kids. Please let your manager know."

My grandkids entered the supermarket with elbows stiff, arms rigid to their sides, feet turned out and hands held out like flippers. Netting over their bodies looked like a cross between feathers and scales; they walked like penguins. Customers laughed, one clapped, and the two checkers gawked, holding up their lines. The kids strutted for their audience with exaggerated flapping of hands. I corralled them.

"I'm going to give each of you four dollars for your dinner. You can choose any candy you want, but you can't go over this dollar limit. Single candy bars are expensive, and stay away from stuff you have to suck on like lemon drops. Any questions?"

"What if we go over four dollars?"

"Then you have to return it or pay for it yourselves."

I pulled two calculators from my pocket and gave one each to Max and Sam. "This will keep you all within your limit. You have to help your younger cousins. You have fifteen minutes, and I'll be waiting at the counter. See that clock behind the pharmacy counter? If you're late, you pay for your own." They waddled to the candy aisle as fast as they could.

I thumbed through body-building and home gardening magazines without the foggiest idea of the content. Max startled me as he shuffled up to my blind side. "Does that four dollars include tax?"

"Uh, uh, no, I'll pay the tax."

Keegan returned from scouting so fast he swung wide into the cracker display because he couldn't lean into the turn. He fumbled to restack the display as he watched his siblings and cousins. He was losing shopping time in the candy aisle.

Second to the produce department, I favor the smell of the candy aisle. I walked down their aisle, listening to their chatter.

"How much does this package of Twix, Gummy Bears and licorice come to?" Jack asked Sam who held a calculator.

"Four dollars and twenty-three cents—too much. You're going to have to trade something back."

They struggled with the concept of eating anything they wanted. I had seen them scared, hungry, or injured, but never this anxious. Lauren wrung her hands as she walked sideways down the aisle with her eyes scanning the shelves. After experimenting with price combinations and watching the clock, they settled on their mishmash of sweets. The stress at check-out was like waiting to receive a report card. Each watched the cash register. Before taxes, the totals ranged from $3.68 to $3.96.

Back in the car I announced the rest of the rules. "You can't trade or give away any of your candy. If you get sick and puke, you have to go to bed and miss the rest of the night. I recommend that you eat slowly and space out what you eat."

"I'm going to eat my KitKats at 5:00," Jack said, "my Twix at 5:30, and save my Reese's Cups until 7:00."

"I'll eat both sacks of Candy Corn and M&M'S right away," Lauren said. "If I don't get sick, I'll eat my Hershey's Kisses for dessert at 8:00."

"If I go outside and throw up, does that count?" Sam asked.

"That would be cheating," Max said.

The sugar high from candy they ate on the way home, combined with anticipation for the evening, meant these kids were pumped. As we neared home, they wiggled out of their nets to be free for more unknown but fun stuff.

ᘒ

Mary described the first event. "You are going to play hide and seek in total darkness in the living room. Whoever is "it" must not only find someone but also identify him or her. I already have your names in a bowl to see who will be "it" first. If someone isn't found, we'll turn on the lights to find that good hider."

Because I lived here, I figured I knew about anywhere a kid could hide. After two rounds they became more innovative. Three crawled in a sleeping bag and twined together like worms. Keegan was "it" when he stumbled across the bag but was unable to locate the zipper handle pulled inside. He could feel their bodies but not distinguish who was who. Technically they weren't caught.

Lauren removed a lamp from an end table and stood in its place. Keegan crawled on top of a high bookcase in a space I had not seen in years. Grant gave up when he couldn't find them. But Jack stopped the game when he couldn't be found behind the screen in the unlit fireplace. When he proudly unfolded himself, he left black footprints on the carpet that were worthy of Bigfoot. The rest of us turned in fear, waiting for Mary's reaction, relieved when she took a breath.

We spent the next half hour vacuuming, scrubbing, and sterilizing the crime scene while Sam contained Mary in the bedroom waiting for her heart to slow down. He opened the door and stuck his head out. "Papa, do you have a paper bag that Nana can breathe into?"

Jack showered and changed into clothes that didn't fit.

"Showtime!" I said. "Now you're going to perform a silent scene with a strobe light, fog machine, and player piano in the background. The villain, Sam, grabs the damsel, Lauren, by her neck and tries to drag her away. The hero, Max, comes to her rescue. In the struggle, Max knocks someone else over, and a barroom fight breaks out. All in slow motion. Each blow must be exaggerated. We have long-sleeved white shirts for all. The flashing strobe will stop the action; white shirts will magnify the action."

"We don't really hit each other, do we?" Keegan asked.

"I get to hit Keegan first," Grant announced.

"Nobody gets hit, nobody gets hurt. So let's practice. Sam, act like you gave me a real hard stomach punch." In slow motion I bent at my waist and threw arms forward with my mouth agape, as though all the wind had been knocked out of me. "Now I turn around and Jack, you give me a roundhouse slug, like you hit me in the jaw. Just tap my jaw, but follow through with your punch." Slowly I turned my head with eyes bugged out, mouth open, and jaw displaced sideways by the blow. "Lauren, you will kick and scream in silence, while waving your arms. Now pick a partner and rehearse some fights. The whole scene will last only a minute or two."

The scene they developed followed their combat video games. They coached each other and continued to build a fight scene a professional wrestler would envy.

"I'm going to turn off the lamps, turn on the strobe light, start the player piano, and yell action. Do whatever you rehearsed. Stop when the music stops."

Imagination and enthusiasm carried the show. The music stopped. Mary and I clapped and hooted. "Bravo! Bravo!"

"Magic, pure magic," Mary said. "All we needed to do was get them kick-started and get out of the way."

"Papa, let's do it again. I have more ideas," Lauren yelled, arms held high to get my attention.

"I can do it better next time," Max said.

"Two more times and that's it, kids. Now show us your stuff. Action!"

∾

Our third event prompted a visit to the kitchen to collect supplies: six twelve-inch-long sections of half-inch PVC pipe for blowguns, sandwich bags on strings for ammo pouches, and protective eye goggles. A marshmallow war loomed on the horizon. The miniatures can fly through the air and travel thirty feet in the blink of an eye.

Mary announced fair warning. "If I catch you running with pipes in your mouth or doing any damage, I'm going to pinch your heads off."

The grandkids divided into two teams: Lauren, Sam and Jack against Max, Keegan, and me. As Grant was too young to pucker and produce an effective blow, he floated wherever the action took him.

Anyone hit with a marshmallow was out. War continued until an entire team was eliminated. When a hit was contested, the shooter made the final call. Mary functioned as referee to settle arguments and declare foul play.

I knew with my maturity and strategy, I could outwit, finesse, and dodge any kid. Our team would overtake the enemy with shock and awe. "Let the games begin!" I announced.

Mary flipped a coin to determine who would go around the corner and down the hall as the defensive team. They moved chairs and squatted behind them, hiding, waiting for an assault from the offense.

While the enemy hid, I explained my strategy to our team. "We'll shoot one blowgun at a time. That way one of us will always have a loaded gun. But if they all shoot at once, we can rush them before they can reload. I will lead, and you two follow me."

We slid into stealth mode. The top of an enemy head bobbed from around a door for a quick scan of our advancing position but disappeared too quickly for us to shoot. We heard whispering. With perfect coordination, heads popped from doors on each side of the hall. Each gun delivered a single accurate shot. Our team was dead in less than one minute in Round One.

In Round Two we hid while the enemy came after us. I figured I could shoot from a closet with the door cracked open only wide enough to expose the gun tip while I peeked with one eye. I was the perfect sniper in the dark. Jack leaned out an open door and shot my hand through the one-inch gap in the door. What I had expected as a learning curve for the kids was instead a vertical line. They never *learned*, they just *did*. I became the least-wanted team member.

In Round Three we advanced and the enemy retreated in an orderly manner. Jack darted from behind a sofa to behind the kitchen counter. Our team got off three late shots behind his moving butt. We were too slow. While we wasted shots on Jack, Lauren and Sam ducked behind kitchen chairs stacked with throw pillows.

What happened? This was not a retreat. This was an ambush. We had been suckered in and surrounded. We filled the air with white streaks, a few aimed but mostly wild desperate shots. Occasionally, we loaded several marshmallows into one gun, then popped them out like a shotgun. Not good for distance or accuracy, but we were hoping for a lucky hit.

My team lost three straight rounds, resulting in a loss of confidence in their self-appointed leader.

We made up rules as we ducked and weaved. Usually we felt the marshmallow strike us. Following several disputed kills, Mary ruled that anyone who contested being hit had to sit out the next round. Ricochets didn't count. After each round, teams gathered replacement ammo from the floor to refill their pouches. A pack of hungry puppies could not have lapped them up faster.

Before restarting the war games, we restructured the teams to level the playing field. My grandkids, though polite and restrained, chose me last. Caught in the open with a marshmallow coming, the kids could usually dodge the bullet. I was the most vulnerable player. Agility, small size, and good eyesight prevailed over strategy which improved as team members used hand signals to communicate.

In Round Four Max quietly pointed out an exposed enemy foot to Keegan and directed him to go around a chair by curving his hand and walking his fingers through the air. Keegan smiled, nodded, and stalked along the opposite side of the hall. All was quiet until the first shot was fired and shouting broke out. "Got you." "Did not." "Shoot now while he's reloading." "He's behind that door." "Watch to your right." "Rush her, she's empty." "Ricochets don't count." "They're coming around the corner, Harold," Mary declared, "and Max got you. You're dead!"

Will they someday get too old to play with me?

❧

After the marshmallow war, we hurried through midnight balloons and horns, grabbed our sleeping bags, and shot out the door to lie in a circle on the trampoline. As soon as the last person found a position, yelling stopped and no one said a word for five minutes. We lay bunched together in sleeping bags looking up at the burnt black sky thick with stars. I wanted them to be conscious of the first five minutes of a new year alone with their private thoughts. Maybe, just maybe, one, or perhaps all of them, would begin each new year with this tradition, and, if the spell worked, it would be passed on to their children.

While kids huddled silently beside me, I wondered if I was euphoric or the stars were actually brighter. I had never before been so acutely aware of the gifts beside me. "For a minute," I said softly, "let's all listen to the sounds of the night, then talk about what we heard."

"Somebody farted," Sam said.

"That's not a night sound," Lauren said.

I tried not to giggle. "Now let's get serious for a few minutes."

Keegan spoke first. "I heard a train a long ways off and a big truck on the interstate."

"Did anyone else hear that owl?" Jack asked.

"I could hear the stars," Lauren said.

"That's crazy," Sam said. "What do stars sound like?"

"When they twinkle, I imagine tinkling bells."

"I heard all those sounds," Max said "I love the sounds on a cold night. Summer sounds are mushy, but winter sounds are crisp and clear."

As my grandkids spoke, their voices softened, dispensed by wind into the dark. "Story time," I said with a full heart. "Sam, you go first."

Sam began our annual extemporaneous story that could be as wild as *Harry Potter* and included ridiculous characters, plots and general nonsense as we stepped inside our imaginations. When he stopped mid-sentence, the next in birth order had to complete the sentence and continue the story from there.

The stars faded beneath a thickening overcast. As though snow were part of our plan, we watched flakes as large as chicken feathers drift onto our faces. With the only flashlight, Sam could spot a huge flake fifteen feet above the trampoline. All eyes focused on the oversized flake until it settled on us. Gravity had to be working at half strength. We opened our mouths like baby birds.

Keegan and Grant elaborated on our stories. We wiggled lower into our bags and cranked up imaginations, continuing with tales as we lay surrounded by the bliss of our once-a-year night together. Then it was I became the protective blanket itself, the ultimate box house, the safe harbor, as I hovered and hugged. The grandkids accepted my behavior as normal.

Running out of stories and warmth, we hurried back to the house with sleeping bags. The kids jockeyed for floor positions to watch movies. Mary and I retreated to a real bed. "You won't believe the stories they made up," I told her. *Alice in Wonderland* would be jealous, and the snow … " Mary's deep rhythmic breathing ended my babbling.

In the morning, our living room resembled an army camp: kids sprawled in and out of their bags. I looked forward to their awakening in our home as they would lighten our day with joy that Mary and I could not duplicate on our own. As we stood talking and taking in the clutter, Max raised his head, blinked his eyes and said, "Hold up a minute, I want to join you." He stepped over three cousins and weaved around two brothers to stand next to us.

We tipped our heads back and sang "Oh, What a Beautiful Morning" loudly out of tune. Keegan scrambled out of his bag, leaned into Lauren's sleeping ear, and sang. Grant burrowed deeper into his bag, but Jack propped his head on his elbow and joined in. Sam sat up, rubbing his eyes with his knuckles.

Our homespun Reveille continued until everyone joined in. Without missing a beat, Lauren mounted a kitchen chair, cupped her left hand behind her ear and, with a wooden spoon for a baton in her right hand, swung ever higher, indicating louder. Grant stuck his head out like a groundhog checking for his shadow, blinked, and joined in.

"Everything's going our way. Happy New Year!"

Grant, Lauren, Keegan in the Marshmallow Wars

Flipping Switches

"Harold, close the front door. You're letting out the heat," my mother yelled one winter day fifty years ago. The previous night's problems had included too much running water in the tub and holding the refrigerator door open too long.

"Mary, turn off those lights behind you," Mary's mother said in another part of the same town about the same time.

I closed the door and Mary turned off the lights because our mothers said so, not because we really understood why. Neither of us understood the relationship between flipping a light switch and paying an unknown person in a distant place.

Twenty-five years later, Mary and I dutifully harangued Lori and Amy who passed on the tradition to their children with the same lesson learned—nothing. Perhaps this is a ritual of blindly following rules until we leave home and discard them, until we begin to pay our own utility bills. I wondered if Mary and I could pass on a valuable lesson earlier in life. Maybe we could alter the cycle of needless badgering.

As grandparents, Mary and I always looked for excuses to have our kids and grandkids come to our house. Our obvious goal was to have fun, but the hidden agenda concerned what we could teach them as a supplement to school, as in a lesson of day-to-day living. We excluded all toy-store products, especially if the toys ran on batteries or did not offer interaction with kids. The evening events did not turn on what we ate, but what we did. Bean-night meals were always quick, easy to prepare and involved minimal clean up.

Mary selected the age-old, dependable, garden-variety pinto beans to soak overnight and cook the next day. As per Mary, every meal required a leafy green and constituted heresy without it: spinach, lettuce, cabbage. The specific green didn't matter.

To six grandkids and their parents, we ladled beans into paper bowls and served cornbread. Conversation included taking turns around the table telling one good event and one bad that happened to each that day. After years of the bean-night ritual, everyone learned to listen to one another.

∾

On a Friday evening in August, crickets clicked in the hot muggy air. Our grandkids, fresh from their first week of school after summer vacation, sat around the table. I leaned forward and cleared my throat. "Wipe your mouths and tell Nana thanks for the beans and cornbread. Take your spoons, glasses, and bowls to the sink, and come back to the table."

Stumbling over each other, they returned quickly and sat staring at me in anticipation. Their silence was scary. With theatrics of a magician, I waved my hand back and forth above my head and reached into a Walmart shopping bag, whereupon I pulled out six sandwich baggies with coins inside. "I'm giving each of you six sacred quarters in a bag. Don't lose it. Follow me out near the trash cans because I have something to show you."

I needed to move the evening's plan along because late August in Tulsa discourages anyone from lingering outside. Daily newspaper reports noted deaths from dehydration and heat. The western sun had already stolen shade from the electric meter box.

∾

Our girls and their spouses knew the plan and watched with curiosity to see how the kids would react to my experiment. The kids followed me out to the side of our house where a wooden fence camouflaged two trash cans and an air conditioner. The adults trailed along. Everyone needed to have a good view of the electric meter secured on our house adjacent to the fence. High enough to be under the overhanging roof but low enough for an adult male to read, it was too high for children to see. I had arranged an aluminum stepladder and folding stepstool next to the wooden rail surrounding the trash cans. If the smaller kids stood on the top steps and the older ones on the lower, all could see the meter.

Max and Sam climbed the ladder first which screwed up my plans. Max squeezed the coin bag in one hand as he climbed with the other, while Sam climbed with two hands, his coin bag stuffed in a pocket.

"Max, you and Sam back off and make room for the smaller ones to climb up and see," I scolded.

The twins climbed down the ladder and everyone jostled for a step to get the best view of the low-tech glass bowl with wheels and gears inside. Wires ran out the top and bottom, disappearing mysteriously into the wall. Keegan climbed up, tripping over untied shoes, and leaned over the rail. Max, Jack, and Lauren, peered from the ladder. Jack, bothered with allergies, needed to blow his nose. Standing on the stepstool, Sam held Grant on his hip.

Computer games program kids to take control and interact, so this simple, silent device baffled them. They did not understand watching a wheel turn, especially if the gadget did not have any buttons to push or knobs to twist. This rotating wheel could not compete with Nintendo, Game Boy, or any down-loadable computer game. I assumed they thought in terms of let's get on with crashing a spaceship or slaying a dragon with a hero's sword. Where was the rocker switch or flashing lights or icons or buttons to be activated? They watched the meter wheel turning, as their heads and eyes rotated in sync.

"What do you think you're watching?" I asked.

The younger ones deferred to the twins.

"I think it's called an electric meter," Max said after a long pause.

"What's it do?" I asked.

"Makes electricity," Jack blurted, wiping his nose with the back of his hand and tapping his finger on the glass.

"That thing's turning," Keegan said as he grasped both sides of the bowl, pulled himself forward and pressed his nose to the glass, eyes still in focus up close as only a child can do.

"Max, count out loud how many times that wheel rotates past the black mark at the top. I'll look at my watch for one minute and tell you when to stop. Ready, GO."

"One, two, three, four … " Max counted.

"STOP."

"Thirty-two," Max said.

"What does that mean?" I said while they continued to watch the wheel rotate.

"How much electricity is being used?" Sam said.

"How can we make it spin faster?" I asked.

They shouted more guesses: "Turn on more lights." "Turn on the TV." "Turn on the computer."

"Let's go do it," I said.

They bolted from their perches like their feet were on fire, exploding into the house, vying to see who could flip the most switches the fastest. I could have held my breath from the time their feet engaged the ground until they resumed their perches.

"Sam, it's your turn to count the revolutions. Ready, GO." The wheel turned faster.

Sam counted faster, "One, two, three, four … "

"STOP."

"Wow, did you see that? We did fifty-four turns," Sam bragged.

"Who made this meter spin faster?" I asked.

"We did," they proudly proclaimed.

"Then who do you think should pay for this increased electricity?" Their silence was as dramatic as their proclamation. I extended my hand, palm up, to each blank-faced kid. "You each owe me seventy-five cents."

They grasped the purpose of the $1.50 in a baggie. One would have thought I was asking to amputate a finger. Disgusted sighs followed as they reached into their bags to pay me seventy-five cents.

"Let's see if we can make the wheel turn faster,"

Challenged to drain more electricity, they stumbled over each other racing inside, forgetting they would be held accountable. The second foraging trip in the house exposed overlooked gadgets that sucked electricity. On went the electric stove, hair dryer, clothes dryer, closet lights, bathroom heater; apparently, there was an unlimited store of electrical switches. This time they required four minutes to do the damage.

They scrambled up the ladder and stood as if their eyeballs were being sucked into the turning wheel.

"Lauren's turn to count," I said.

"Sixty-seven," she yelled.

I held out my hand. "That will be another seventy-five cents from each of you." Now their bags were empty, and I had all the money.

"That's not fun," Lauren said with a pouting lower lip.

As they milled about, I gave them time to digest the events. "I'll make a deal with you. If you can slow that meter below thirty-two revolutions, like we started, I'll give fifty cents back to each of you."

Their first reaction had been glacier slow compared to their response to this new challenge. All six clogged the back door. They shoved, shouted, and accused until the body jam broke and spilled across the floor. The hyper-charged gang spread through the house and flipped off familiar switches: table lamps, wall switches, nightlights. As in hunting Easter eggs, the youngest kid is either too late or can't locate a prize so Grant followed Max around the house.

I followed them inside looking for more change in a dish but had trouble distinguishing the coins in the darkness. Sam witnessed me turning on a lamp. "Papa, turn out that light. You're burning up my money."

They were more concerned that their siblings and cousins might beat them back to the ladder than locating more switches. Promptly, they resumed their positions and fixated eyes on the meter.

"Jack's turn to count," I said. This time the slower rotations were obvious.

"Eighteen," Jack shouted. "You owe us fifty cents."

I paid with a hidden grin. "There's another fifty cents in it if you can lower the number below fifteen."

They knew the routine and spread through the house with military precision searching for new targets, looking behind chairs, tables, beds.

"Can we include the garage?" Max asked. "I saw a battery charger for your drill and that thing that sucks up dust from your workbench."

"Sure. That's part of the house."

The energized pack laid siege on the meter and claimed their prior positions. No one waited for a turn but counted in unison.

"Papa, do you see that? Ten! You owe each of us fifty cents," Sam announced.

Now each had all but fifty cents back. Although I was satisfied, I couldn't leave the process alone and decided to push the plan. I announced with self-imposed authority, "If you can get the revolutions under ten, I'll give you the remaining fifty cents." Silently congratulating my cocky self, I was sure it couldn't be done.

The kids searched the house again, held a conference, and sent Lauren out. "Can we turn off the air conditioner?"

Mary and I huddled on that question. We couldn't ask them to decrease electrical use by tying their hands, so we said yes, and broke out lawn chairs in the shade for the adults, waiting for the kids to return. One last time they swept the house like FBI agents, looking for any lights, however small.

Confusion reigned when six pairs of kids' eyes stared to see whether or not the wheel had stopped. By now the adults surrounded the kids, straining on our toes to see the results.

"What's it say?" Amy asked, trying to see over the kids.

"Yeah, what's it say?" Lori asked.

Following hold-your-breath watching, Max softly announced, "Two."

"Two," whispered Mary. "I didn't think it was possible."

I dispensed the final fifty cents to each in silence. The kids scurried off, satisfied with their victory.

∽

Two weeks later Lori called. "Hi, Daddy. I thought you would like to know I saw Jack explaining our electric meter to a neighbor friend."

I learned the kids would listen if the project was fun, they were actively involved, and I didn't repeat myself—the most difficult point to remember. To my surprise I discovered our refrigerators drained the greatest amount of electricity. The old one in the garage I had refused to throw away was history.

Now drawn to glance at the speed of our meter whenever I pass, if I'm at a friend's home, I also peek at the speed of theirs.

Hats on Stage

"**M**ary, where are the old overalls I paint in?" Those bibs were aged and comfortable, like an old friend. I saved them with their splotches of color over the years for function, not fashion.

"I remember seeing the goofy-looking things somewhere on a closet shelf," Mary said. "This is a good time to throw them away if I find them." She opened the front closet. "Harold, come here. I want to show you something. You're not going to believe this."

She pulled out hats from back shelves and handed them to me. "I remember this one," she said, "and this one, but where did the crushed Russian one come from? Can you believe the number of hats we've collected? Looks like they've been breeding in the dark closet."

"Yeah, and weird ones look like they've crossbred and mutated. You're not tall enough to see in the back of that next shelf," I said. I stood on my toes and groped along the back of the shelf, pulling out more crumpled hats, some stuffed inside of others. Fortunately, my hat tricks didn't include rabbits or any undesirable critters.

Mary tried on a Sherlock Holmes deerstalker. "I remember storing some in a box but thought they were in the attic. Simple deduction, Watson, they're in here. Those in the attic must be historic Fourth of July hats."

I put on a Russian hat and followed up with a couple of squats and kicks but couldn't get up without grabbing a chair. I should have picked an easier hat.

"Yodel-Ay-Ee-Oooo," Mary said, dramatically pushing me aside as she donned an Austrian hat with a feather in its brim.

We forgot about the overalls.

"Where does this stuff come from, and why have we saved it?" I asked. Before I finished the question, I deduced the answer. That's what mothers do, in case kids can use the hats in plays, Scouts, or Halloween. Mary saved every scrap of our kids' information, including dismissal information from the hospital when they were born. From that document forward, she stored everything that Lori and Amy brought home, ranging from grade cards to copies of their first drivers' licenses. We traced a few hats back to parties, school plays, and holidays.

"Look what just happened," Mary said. "When we put on a hat, we were transformed. Without hats, you wouldn't have squatted and kicked, and I wouldn't have felt the need to yodel."

"Gives me an idea," I said, ideas whirring faster than our electric meter. "Our grandkids are much more imaginative than we could ever be. Our next bean night, let's see what they can do if they put on these hats."

"Have they lived long enough to know what the hats represent?" Mary asked.

"Let's find out."

"I could hang some sheets as a curtain in the doorway to the living room. Give it more drama."

"Yeah, and they could put on a hat and step around the curtain."

We wanted our grandkids to be comfortable and confident with themselves by being introduced to a friendly audience: their parents, Mary and me. Perhaps someday they could be in a school play or be called on to speak in front of their peers. With any luck, goofy hats might enable them to gather up the courage to be someone or something else.

Cavemen crept out of their caves in camouflage. Masquerade gave fighting tribes, invading armies or comedians the courage to face the enemy on the battlefield or on a stage. Costumes allowed people to access another person's mind and become that character. Free of fear, the actor transformed into someone larger and braver than himself.

"Can they do it?" I asked. "Can they become another character?"

"What if they put on a hat and stand there not knowing what to say?" Mary said.

"If we embarrass them, they'll never forget how we made them feel."

"Especially in front of their parents. The whole idea could be a bust."

"Yeah, and *we* set up their kids to fail. We could even scare or scar them with a bad experience," I said.

Trying to salvage the project, I fumbled for a profound philosophical answer but only came up with, "If the first kid balks, the party's over."

I called their parents and told them what we had in mind for the next bean night. Both families agreed after a pause in which I swear I heard them look at each other, shrug their shoulders, and roll their eyes.

Mary jumped into the conversation on the extension. "Look through your stuff and bring any hats from your house, especially if the kids have a favorite. We need all the props we can find."

"Hide the hats in your trunk when you come over for bean night. Mary will take care of the beans and cornbread as usual," I added.

On Friday night the grandkids laughed and jostled with each other, unconcerned about the evening's activities. Their reactions were consistent with our goals of having them feel safe, happy and fun at Nana's and Papa's house even if the evening was unpredictable.

"Nana," Max said, getting Mary's attention, "you got a surprise for us tonight?"

"Yeah," Lauren said, "are we going to make any money tonight?"

"I know all about the cost of electricity," Sam said.

Satisfied all were finished eating, I pushed back my paper bowl, announced "Showtime," and wiped up crumbs and drippings from the table, while Mary walked around with an open trash bag.

"Drop your bowls, spoons, napkins, and cups in this bag," she said. "You're going to use the table for your show. While we're getting it ready, you kids go outside until we call you. Don't come in unless you're bleeding."

Not knowing what to expect from Mary and me, the younger ones turned to the twins for their leadership. Sam headed for the back door with Max two steps behind, followed by the other four as though they were tied together.

With the help of Doug and Kevin, Mary mounted an old sheet over a spring-loaded rod as a stage curtain in the living room. The Stewart and King parents snuck their hat collections in through the garage. We bent and fluffed long-stored hats, trying to revive them: Daniel Boone's coonskin hat, an African safari hat, a lady's veiled hat from the Roaring Twenties. The kaleidoscope of hats spilled off the dining table onto chairs.

Amy opened the back door. "You kids can come in now, but wipe off any blood before you enter. You *are* the show."

Six grandkids stood before me in the living room. "Nana made a curtain and there's your stage." With a dramatic sweep of my hand, I showed the actors how to push back the curtain and take one step forward to stand on the miniature stage. "Turn around and look at the hats on the table and chairs."

Confused and bewildered, the kids gathered about the table and gawked at the mess of hats.

"You pick a hat, any hat, and stand behind the curtain until you hear Doug's toy drum roll. I'll introduce you. You'll step forward and say something, anything that comes to mind while wearing your hat. It's okay to simply make a silly face. I'll flip a coin to see which one of the twins goes first, then you take turns in birth order."

Max called heads, but tails came up. Sam was first.

The kids continued to stare at the hats. Lauren looked for the door, Max pushed his hands deeper in his pockets, and Jack took a step back. The younger ones didn't move.

Lori coached Sam from the audience. "Pick a hat, Sam. You're first. Just put one on. You'll know what to say."

"When you put on the hat, it'll tell you what to say," I said, trying to be clever and break the stalemate.

The parents leaned forward trying to help. The next few moments determined the destiny for our evening. Mary and I exchanged glances. We needed relief. We needed action.

Unaware that this was the pivotal moment when we might call off the event, Sam reached for the cowboy hat as though it were the only hat on the table. Before he could adjust the hat on his head, five other arms reached out and retrieved hats quicker than a frog's tongue on a bug. The kids lined up behind the curtain in birth order.

As the self-appointed Master of Ceremonies, I stepped on the stage, about the size of a card table. Pausing long enough to build suspense for the crowd of five, like a circus barker I announced, "Laaadies and gentlemen of this esteemed audience, our first act is… (Doug rattled off a drum roll as I pulled back the curtain) … Saaam Stewart!"

Sam strode out onto the stage. With a furrowed brow and a wide-brimmed cowboy hat resting on his ears, he stuck a thumb on either side of his belt buckle, leaned his head back, and sang "Home on the Range," his legs bowed and swaying left and right in time with the music. He paused, grinned, and with his right hand grasped the hat by the front brim, gave a deep bow, and swung the hat low and slow across his knees, milking the audience. Sam ended his performance by flashing an ear-to-ear smile for us.

This first act ignited the small audience of six until we sounded like fifty, stomping our feet, clapping and hooting. The other kids caught the excitement and wanted their turn. We had momentum. Mary flashed a grin across the room to me and winked. We did it.

"We have searched world-wide for our next act," I said. "I present to you … (drum roll) … Maaax Stewart!"

With a tall black hat, deep voice, and right index finger in the air, Max spoke. "Four Score and seven years ago, our fathers brought forth on this continent, a new nation, conceived in liberty, and dedicated to the proposition that all men are created equal ... etcetera, etcetera." He paused for effect. "And that government of the people, by the people, for the people, shall not perish from the earth." His smile matched his twin brother's smile.

"Bravo! Bravo! More! Very good!" yelled the audience.

The first actors ran to grab different hats and joined the back of the line.

"Our next actor is none other than the beautiful, delightful ... (drum roll) ... Laaauren King!"

Lauren stuck out her head from behind the curtain, acting as though scared. She scanned the room and stepped out with hesitation. In her left arm an old gray felt hat was rolled up like a thick newspaper twisted on one end to vaguely resemble a head. She stroked the head with her right hand. Looking slowly back and forth over our heads, searching, she said, "Toto, this doesn't look like Kansas."

Six adults exceeded the maximum noise allowed in a city residence. Energized by enthused feedback, Lauren rushed to grab another hat and rejoin the line.

The kids' minds were on fire as they pulled dramatic characters out of hats. Thoughts like sparklers backlit their eyeballs. The new question was not which hat to grab, but which hat for the next round.

"Our next actor is ... (drum roll) ... Jaaack Stewart!"

So excited for his turn, Jack pulled back the curtain behind me before I completed his introduction. He wore a Revolutionary War tricorn hat, paused long enough for the audience to stop talking, and blurted out with a strong voice, "I cannot tell a lie. I chopped down the," he began exiting the stage, "cherry tree." While we cheered, his mind was on another hat with a skit to match.

Caught up in the excitement, I took the stage. "Ladies and gentlemen, as you can tell, our actors are experienced and have delivered their lines eloquently. The actors continue to be clever, original, and over-the-top performers. There is more to come. Our next act comes straight from Hollywood. I present to you … (drum roll) … Keeegan King!"

Keegan donned a silver party hat resembling a funnel upside down on his head. He moved his shoulders and elbows. "Squeak, squeak, rattle, rattle. I'm off to see the wizard on the Yellow Brick Road. He's going to give me a heart or maybe a brain. I can't remember." Walking across the small stage with short "squeaking" steps, he disappeared behind the curtain to spirited applause.

Five-year-old Grant required help. Sam picked out a pirate's hat for him, adjusted the hat and an eye patch, and rehearsed lines with him. "Ladies and gentlemen," I said, "our next actor straight off a pirate's boat is … (drum roll) … Graaant King."

The elastic string on his eye patch was overstretched, causing the patch to rest on Grant's cheek. Excited to deliver his lines, he never knew the difference. His hat sat so low, he had to tilt his head back to see. "I'll make you walk the plank," he said, remaining on stage with his head tilted back while Max coached. While the audience yelled and clapped, Kevin stood and punched the air. The remaining adults joined him with a standing ovation. Meanwhile, the kids applauded each other and patted the younger ones on their backs.

The hat supply lasted two more rounds with some hats used more than once for different characters with new scripts. The third round revealed their extensive exposure to Saturday morning cartoons, which supplied an unlimited number of oddball characters. To think Mary and I were concerned about getting them to put on a show. Now we didn't know how to diplomatically bring it to a conclusion.

"That's it, kids," I announced reluctantly. "You need to wrap it up. We're getting hoarse and our hands are sore. Keegan, you'll be last." I pulled back the curtain. "Our final actor is … (drum roll) … Keeegan King."

Keegan stepped boldly from behind the curtain, clad in a tan baseball cap turned backward, which made him look bald. He pulled both ears forward with his index fingers and pushed up his nose with his thumb. "Th - th - th - that's all folks."

∽

As the parents gathered their kids and headed for home, Mary and I stacked up hats to be stored and again forgotten. I paused examining the hats, picking up one while staring at another. They spoke to me. "I wanted to grab a hat and get in line," I told Mary. "M-i-c-k-e-y M-o-u-s-e," I sang beneath giant black ears.

No sooner did I sit down when Mary placed a tiara on her head. "Where are my knights to protect me?" She moved to a chair as an audience of one and indicated it was my turn. "Break a leg."

Donning a Smokey the Bear campaign hat, I stepped on stage. "Only you can prevent forest fires," I said with a lame vocal imitation and sat down.

"Smokey, only you can prevent forest fires, but you can start a fire in my forest," Mary said with a sly grin.

"Ahem!" Our firstborn stood gawking at us. "I forgot my purse and let myself in the garage door. I didn't expect to interrupt a second act by the grandparents."

Mary and I watched Lori pick up her purse and close the door behind herself. As we stared in embarrassment at the closed door, she reopened it and stuck her head back in. "The fire extinguisher is in the hall closet." She pointed to the closet. "Don't forget I grew up here."

Play Well

"The good fairy left another box of Legos on the front porch," Mary said as she stepped inside with the morning paper.

I shook my head. "Amy and Kevin took me seriously when I said we would take all the Legos they could find. Looks like I shot my mouth off."

Early in Amy and Kevin's marriage, they developed into master garage-sale shoppers. Reading Saturday morning addresses, they screened high-value areas, driving slowly past sales to determine potential.

Their kids were running through soccer shoes and sports clothes. Amy bought all sizes and colors. At least one kid could usually find shoes and clothes to fit before another grew into them. Kevin screened for electronics that needed but batteries to reap their true value on eBay.

Foraging through goods, they frequently came across boxes full of large-size Legos. A shoebox full sold for twenty-five cents and a full kitchen trashcan, seventy-five cents. The retail value of individual sets would have been between forty and fifty dollars. Over the course of a year, the Kings delivered enough Legos to fill a bathtub, at a total cost to me of less than twenty dollars.

As my stockpile grew, I found myself grinning, then dipping and running my hand through the Legos, palm up, fingers splayed like a pirate running fingers through his booty of gold. Even as a kid, I could not imagine this many toys to fondle and stack. Delayed gratification was paying off.

Store-bought toys in my childhood consisted of Tinkertoys or an Erector Set. Tinkertoys were quick to assemble, but, with extended playtime, the wooden pieces loosened and fell apart. The aluminum Erector Set never fell apart, wore out or disintegrated. With all the nuts and bolts, a kid needed the patience of Job to follow the step-by-step assembly of a complex machine or working toy illustrated in the booklet of plans. I developed the patience to follow directions, but then what? A kid was held hostage to the booklet; the parts were not conducive to originality or imagination.

Legos wouldn't fall apart or wear out and offered tools for imaginations young and old. Our hoard of rectangular-shaped, interlocking Lego bricks was dominated by bright yellow, red, and green, with a few scatterings of purple, white, pink, and black. We were fortunate to also have bricks two to four times longer than regular Legos. These prized bricks were desirable for spanning gaps like doors, bridges, and roofs.

Since the Legos were purchased from garage sales, the original boxes were long gone, as were the booklets for models. Using their imagination, the grandkids played and experimented, building simple four-sided walls and forts. As we accumulated more Lego bricks, their fortifications expanded proportionally. Storage became a problem. We stacked large plastic bins of Legos in closets behind clothes and high up on shelves.

Mary finally said, "Harold, we're out of space. Enough Legos!"

◌◡◌

"Nana is in a good mood today," I said to the kids, "and says we can have her kitchen for two days to build while you spend two nights with us over spring break."

"Why the kitchen?" Lauren asked.

"Because the countertops are a good firm surface to build on."

"What do we build?" Max asked.

"You're going to build a city, and each of you will have three feet of space on the countertop. You can negotiate and interlock with your neighbor for something fancy or just build up next to him or her. You have to connect the counters with bridges and span doorways so we can duck in and out. You'll build a bridge over the sink and get past the refrigerator by using a stool as a single pillar for a bridge. We'll store Legos around the room, so pick what you need as you work, especially colors."

"What's it supposed to look like?" Lauren asked.

"That's up to you. Use your imagination and the colors for patterns, like trimming a door or window. You'll have forty-eight hours, beginning at 1:00 p.m. on Thursday.

Too young to participate, Grant wandered around while the five older kids worked like contractors staying up late and rising early to get a jump on the competition, as if there were a late penalty clause. No penalty, but there would be a prize. Mary would judge the buildings on originality of purpose and design; the winner would accompany me to Blockbuster to choose two movies for Saturday afternoon.

Mary could only open the refrigerator enough to reach milk for breakfast and ingredients for sandwiches. We brought in other food as needed.

Without instructions or plans, they experimented, failed, and modified until they were satisfied. Stubborn pride kept them from seeking consultations with a sibling or cousin, other than giving a helping hand to the younger ones.

Their buildings grew three feet tall with spiked towers and minarets reaching near the ceiling, enough to block the cabinet doors. Color patterns covered the walls of their buildings, some resembling mosaic tiles. To build a fire escape, Jack turned bricks sideways protruding from the wall making steps that zigzagged down the front of his building. Intense negotiations regarding architectural patterns and colors enabled them to blend with their neighbors. Each building had its own personality filling the allotted space. Lauren added to her landscape by using some of Mary's artificial flowers.

By 1:00 p.m. Saturday, they continued to modify, adjust and align doors and windows, while talking with food in their mouths.

"That's all, kids," I said. "Quit! Stop! Time's up."

"Papa, just a few more minutes," Jack said. "Mine's not as high as Sam's."

"That's it," Mary said, waving her arms as though stopping traffic. After announcing the winner, she said, "I want my kitchen back. Take some photos to show your parents and clear my kitchen."

Reluctantly, the kids disassembled their proud creations in chunks as big as possible.

༄

"See those five piles of Legos on the floor?" I said to the five oldest grandkids. They nodded. "Each of you gets sixty Legos to build a bridge on the floor—a strong bridge. Don't worry about using pretty colors, concentrate on strength. You have fifteen minutes until we test your bridge, which must span at least twelve inches."

"That's not very big," Max mumbled.

I pulled out a ruler. "We'll test each bridge by stacking three food cans on it. If your bridge holds up, we'll move the three cans to the next bridge. We'll add another can for the second round and continue adding until the last bridge falls or is left standing."

"Mine will be the strongest," Lauren said, taunting the boys.

"We'll just see," Max said.

Sam scooped up his pile and moved to the hall for his secret architectural bridge design. Max moved his bricks to a kitchen corner for privacy.

Keegan's bridge fell before he completed the span. Frustrated, he ran around the corner to see Sam's, then looked at Max's design.

"Papa," Max yelled, trying to hide his bridge design as he hovered in a squat with both arms and hands out and his back to Keegan, "come and get Keegan. He's cheating."

As they stacked bricks in a frenzy, I walked around monitoring their progress and measuring their bridge spans with the ruler. I assisted Keegan since he was the youngest bridge builder.

"Time's up!"

Keegan tested his bridge first by stacking three cans of Jolly Green Giant Beans on it pyramid-style. When his bridge did not fall, we moved the same three cans to the next kid. Each kid placed the testing cans with finesse as though they would detonate. No bridges fell.

For Round Two, I added a can of Ranch Style Beans. Every bridge tolerated the weight. Round Three included a can of Hunt's Diced

Tomatoes. Keegan's bridge went first. To move the process along, I upped the ante and added a quart of mayonnaise.

"What in the world are you doing with that glass jar?" Mary said in a loud scolding voice. "If that breaks, all of you will be cleaning up glass and mayonnaise for a week."

I flinched along with the kids, and they all looked at me. "Bad decision," I said, putting the mayonnaise back on the shelf in favor of adding Morton Salt to the bridges.

Jack's bridge collapsed with the addition of a second can of Ranch Style Beans and Lauren's fell with Campbell's Cream of Chicken Soup. Both Sam and Max built bridges reinforced from the sides, which added additional anchoring at the stress points, but Max's bridge crumbled after the addition of two cans of Campbell's Cream of Mushroom Soup. Sam's bridge alone stood in the hall with ten cans stacked and teetering.

"I want to see how strong my bridge is," Sam whispered.

Because we all wondered about the breaking point, I looked through our pantry and found an unopened ten-pound sack of sugar. "Sam, it's your bridge to test," I said. "Remove all the cans and see if you can balance that sack of sugar on your bridge." Even Grant stood still as the rest of us tiptoed and talked in whispers. Sam's bridge stood the sugar-sack test.

Mary started clapping, happy not to have mayonnaise and sugar spilled on the floor.

∽

By investing my weekends with the kids, we learned more about stress angles and color schemes. Projects expanded in size and complexity until we built a one-room house about the size of a card table with a pitched roof. Three small kids, a gooseneck lamp, and the reluctant family cat squeezed inside. We turned off the overhead lights. When the kids turned on the lamp, the Lego house glowed as if it were made of stained-glass.

∽

With six months of building behind us, we looked for more specific and challenging projects. Showered with seemingly unlimited Legos, I felt obliged to use all the bricks lest they be taken away. The Legos consumed so much space in our house, even when everyone helped put them away, that Mary and I walked over and around them during the day and sometimes on them in the dark. They were evolving from fun to nuisance. Eventually, I would need to move on without the toys I never had as a child, as well as without my grandkids as playmates. We had learned how to "play well," the translation of the Danish word, "Lego."

"As long as you kids play with them and keep them off the floor, we can leave them out," Mary said, "but when the day comes that the fun wears thin, they're out of here."

❧

My scheduling conflicts, poor weather, or a grandkid's activities meant I sometimes spent more time with one grandkid than another. I then felt obliged to dedicate more time to another grandkid, and so it happened with Keegan in the sixth grade, due to spend the weekend with Mary and me. I called him up. "Keegan, I want you to grab a pen and write this down. Capital E-i-f-f-e-l, space, capital T-o-w-e-r. If you can't find the Eiffel Tower on the Internet, ask one of your parents to help. Learn all about it and be able to tell me. That's what we're going to build when you stay with us next weekend."

"How big?" Keegan knew that building the tower would be a major project based on our other endeavors.

"Look at several views and you decide. We'll have to use the master bedroom because the ceiling is vaulted. I don't figure we can build it during a single weekend."

I selected the Eiffel Tower because millions of people have marveled over it through the years. By building it together, we could both learn the history. Also, Legos were ideal for such a dramatic architectural structure.

When Amy delivered Keegan on Friday after school, he came with eleven computer-generated photos of different angles of the Eiffel

Tower. He also arrived well-informed of its history, architect, recognition, and impact on Paris. He proceeded to give me an overview.

"Where do we start?" I asked.

"Since Legos are bright and the real tower is dark, we have to make it colorful. Let's separate the colors first."

True of all projects, a team must do the grunt work. Separating colors into stacks qualified. Lori dropped Jack off to help sort. I could only squat or sit cross-legged for a short time while separating colors before I needed to stand and move. Sorting required over half an hour with the three of us working continuously before Jack went home.

"How big are you going to build the base?" I wanted to stimulate Keegan's decisions about how big the base of the tower should be relative to the ceiling height of our bedroom. I wanted him to take ownership.

Keegan laid out some of the photos he had brought, looked at the ceiling, looked at the distance between the tower legs, and gathered four red Legos. Without deferring to me, he placed the four bricks on the floor representing the four corners. He backed up, looked at the ceiling, studied a photograph, and moved the bricks out another three inches, about the size of a card table. "There. That looks right for me," he said with confidence.

I never approached my grandkids in an accusatory manner, never embarrassed them, but instead tried to nudge them along. "How do you know you positioned the Lego corners in a square and not a trapezoid or rectangle? If you don't have right angles in the corners, the arches forming the four legs won't fit together."

Walking slowly around the four corner bricks, Keegan looked at me with a blank expression, then back at the bricks. I left him alone to wrestle with the answer while I checked the mail. Fifteen minutes later he was sitting on the floor with his legs crossed, staring at the four bricks. "Papa, I need some string and a Magic Marker," he said with a solemn expression.

I returned with a spool of kite string and cut off two pieces to his satisfaction. With string as a guide, he measured and marked another to the exact length. Placing the strings in an X, he adjusted the opposing corners to match the string. Using another string knotted into four equal lengths around the perimeter, he jockeyed the corner bricks until all were equidistant.

I helped but waited for him to make the decisions. He taped photographs on chairs around our work area as points of reference. Keegan studied the arches and built a temporary scaffolding of books until the blue arching legs interlocked and could stand on their own. His color scheme highlighted the tower's height. Enclosed red stairs worked their way up between levels.

At 8:15 p.m. we stopped for the night after we had completed the first floor, but he couldn't rest easy until confirming the bricks interlocked well and his tower was safe for the night.

Saturday morning found him up working quietly at 6:00 a.m. at the foot of our bed. He was trying to build with limited light without waking Mary or me. Lauren arrived at 9:00 to help, and Jack strolled in an hour later. By Sunday evening, they had completed the first level.

Keegan lived only ten minutes away, so he bummed easy rides to work on his tower Monday and Wednesday evenings to get in three hours of construction. He spent the next three weekends with us, working after school on Fridays through Sunday afternoons.

To reach higher levels, he used a stool and eventually a six-foot aluminum folding stepladder. A month of work finished the project. The final tower reached nine and a half feet, topped off with a homemade French flag taped to a matchstick.

I anticipated his reluctance to dismantle the tower, so before construction began, we agreed to keep it up for one month following completion. Amy, brought him by on weekends so he could walk around the tower and admire his work. Occasionally he adjusted a Lego brick or changed out an easy color and brought friends over to prove his construction story. Other times he sat on the floor gazing at his work.

რ

Two years later, Grant was over one afternoon. "Papa, would you help me build something big like you did with Keegan?"

"Sure. I would like that. Do you remember the rules? Number one: we finish the building no matter how long it takes. Number two: you have to know all about whatever you build. Number three: we don't have the TV on when building."

For the next two months, we thumbed through magazines, watched TV, and explored the Internet. Together we settled on the Golden Gate Bridge. Grant was a year younger than Keegan was when he built the Eiffel Tower. With my assistance, we copied photos from the computer from many angles and learned the history of the bridge.

Like his big brother, he wanted to stay with us on weekends to work on his project. The Eiffel Tower required height but minimal space. The Golden Gate Bridge, however, required space, lots of space. To complicate the issue, we knew from experience that floor space would be occupied for a minimum of a month after completion. We settled on the space from one side of our master bed extending down the hall. Furthermore, we couldn't determine the length needed on each end for the approach roads until we completed the two main towers. Keeping the two towers and suspension in proportion was important. We estimated our need to be a minimum of twenty-five feet.

For the next five weekends, Grant followed the house rules until we finished. The real bridge hung on cables which could not be duplicated with Legos, so we employed bright red kite string for the cables. We built the bridge towers to scale, frequently referencing photos taped about the bedroom.

As construction progressed, Mary learned how to walk down the hall with handfuls of laundry and step back and forth over his prized bridge. One end of the bridge and highway approach even ran along her side of the bed.

❧

Mary demonstrated her patience with our projects, fixed our meals, and stepped over scattered ankle-twisting Legos for weeks on end, happily appreciating the presence of our grandkids.

The grandkids understood we could not complete a project in thirty minutes, insert two batteries and return to the TV. They learned the long process would be rewarded with pride and the satisfaction of completion. With Legos as bait, Mary and I were more fun than their friends, and I enjoyed having playmates.

❧

We played with the Legos less and less as the twins entered high school and the younger ones became involved with school activities. Old-fashioned large-brick Legos were being replaced by smaller components and superheroes. Months eased into years, and the kids came more to swim or play on the trampoline rigged with a safety harness and giant bungee. Patterns emerged whereby they brought their own playmates and I watched.

I sat at the breakfast table drinking coffee. "Mary, they're outgrowing us."

"That's a good problem to have." She apparently did not know the origin of my thought behind the statement, about losing my playmates, and didn't push me to explain.

"Storage of all those Legos is getting to be a nuisance," I said. "I'm ready to give them to Amy and Kevin for their school fundraising garage sale."

"I've been wishing you would give them up," she said with a sympathetic pat on my head as she refilled my cup and ran her hand down the back of my neck.

Grant's Lego Golden Gate Bridge

Dream Running

A gentle wind washes over me. My heart beats fast, not from fear but from anticipation. Running faster and faster, I leap like Superman over driveways, streets, cars, bushes, trees, and backyards. With eyes and head tilted far back, I look up into the cloudless blue sky. The more I stretch and arch my back to soar, the more time I have to smell the morning. Full control. Ahhh. So neat, so sweet. As I somersault in slow motion, I watch the green lawn approaching. Landing on the ground I bend my knees and leap to fly again.

My focus is not height, speed, or distance, but grace. Each soaring somersault is higher and more graceful than the last. I never plan my next move, just let it happen. But something is wrong. The last two landings make me flinch. I rouse myself awake from this entrancing state and pull the covers over my eyes in a vain effort to recapture the dream and fly again, but I have to pee.

Which are more creative? Sleeping dreams or daydreams?

With thousand-yard stares out a window during seventh-grade history class, I try to conjure up and resuscitate dreams from the night before. A forced dream doesn't work so I apply thought to paper by drawing sequential stick figures running across a yard, leaping ever higher and farther. These leaps require a lot of Big Chief pages taped side by side into a foldout. By doing this, I discover I can program my sleeping dreams. A breakthrough! A new era opens for me. Of course this diverts my concentration and energy from class. I daydream from Plymouth Rock to the Civil War.

As decades drift by, my exhilarating dreams of flight appear less frequently. Amy rekindles them when she becomes an outstanding gymnast. Instead of leaping in my dreams, I watch her in person. She progresses from a series of six to seven to eight quick, crisp back handsprings. With increasing speed across the floor, she ends with a beautiful, tightly-tucked back somersault, landing on her feet with arms held high, chin up, and a smile on her face. Just as I had in my dreams. I fly and tumble with her through the air and clap the loudest.

Once again, I begin leaping in my dreams. I don't wish to duplicate her lightning-fast handsprings lasting but seconds and ending abruptly like a knife spinning through the air and sticking into a tree. What she accomplishes in gymnastics doesn't fit my dreams of slowly drifting, rotating, and landing with grace. Her moves are akin to tap dancing, mine to waltzing in the sky. Her goal, an objective high score; mine, personal fulfillment.

∽

Before Grant grew too big, I rented a small tank of helium from the party store. The grandkids and I experimented with twelve-inch balloons. To our surprise, a single helium-filled party balloon lifted only one paperclip. Six balloons could lift only six paperclips. The answer to more lift was not more twelve-inch balloons, but larger ones. The next week, Jack and I bought four three-foot-diameter balloons and rented another tank of helium from a party store.

"Hey, Jack, let's show the family what we're going to do and how safe the experiment is going to be."

We stopped by Amy and Kevin's house to pick up Lauren, Keegan, and Grant. Without invitation, we rolled the tank of helium into their kitchen and proceeded to blow up a three-foot balloon. Adults and kids gathered to watch. Within seconds an argument commenced.

"Papa, that's three feet," Lauren said.

I was too close to the balloon to gauge its diameter.

"Stop right there while I get the tape measure," Kevin said, leaning back with caution.

Jack measured. "Two feet, nine inches. I think that's enough."

"If this is a three-foot balloon, we should fill it to three feet," I said as the self-appointed authority on how to fill a helium balloon.

180

"Stop!" Jack yelled. "That's three feet, two inch … "

POW! The balloon didn't pop, it exploded. Their family dog yelped and ran behind the couch, Keegan fell off a kitchen bar-stool, Amy and Lauren screamed while the rest of us stood transfixed. Exploding latex slapped my forehead, creating a blood blister on one side and breaking skin on the other. I staggered backward with both ears ringing. Others close to the balloon gave startled yells and sucked up the freed helium, then jabbered like cartoon characters.

Amy gave a double thumbs up. "Yeah, that's good and safe. You kids go on over to Nana and Papa's tonight, but watch Papa real close."

On our front lawn, we blew up another three-foot balloon and attached it to Grant's belt. One balloon did nothing.

I turned to the Internet to educate myself regarding lift and volume formulas for helium balloons ranging from six to twenty feet in diameter. Even in a light breeze, a balloon that size required a crew. Twenty-one websites later, I narrowed my options to one vender. I settled on six-foot diameter balloons, the size car dealers use with banners attached. Color options were as varied as a starter set of crayons.

After the balloon explosion in the King home, the slap and cut on my forehead, the loss of helium, the failure to launch Grant, and, most of all, the embarrassing loss of credibility with the parents, the arrival of new balloons gave me a chance to redeem myself. I had to get it right this time. When the bright balloons arrived, I was so excited I wanted to call the kids, who were, of course, in school.

The Internet showed me how to calculate the number of cubic feet in a ball and how much weight a cubic foot could lift. The voluminous information provided me with theory but was of limited practical use. Unable to judge a three-foot balloon, how would I be able to tell when a balloon expanded to six feet? How much could one balloon lift? I needed a kid to help me. Max and Sam were unconscious with teenage Saturday morning sleeping sickness, and Jack had a scouting commitment, so I called Lauren. "Honey, I really need your help. I can pick you up right away. Check with your mom." Lauren stood by my side as I explained my plan to Mary. "We're going to blow up a six-foot balloon with a leaf blower in our living room." I heard Mary's eye-roll that said she did not approve but would tolerate my scheme. "There's too much wind outside. We need to pre-stretch the balloons and make sure there are no holes or weak spots."

Mary stepped back, shoulders high and palms up, in surrender. She had made a decision not to become directly involved in our projects because she wanted the bond to be between me and the grandkids. She supported us in the background by always having dinner on the table, running our errands, and picking up and delivering the kids, giving us ample opportunity to play and dream.

Lauren and I pulled on safety glasses, tied two PVC pipes vertically to the back of chairs, and adjusted the pipes exactly six feet apart. She was to stand back, watch the balloon expand between the poles, and indicate with her hands how much space remained on each side. Sitting on the floor between the two poles with a leaf blower, I began filling the balloon. We couldn't talk or even yell above a leaf blower that roared like a jet plane in the living room. Lauren brought her hands closer together until they touched, then we gradually let out the air so the balloon couldn't damage our furnishings.

I talked Keegan into going with me to rent another tank of helium for use in the alley behind the party store. In the alley we cautiously balanced the cylinder on a level surface. With the same PVC pipes Lauren and I used at home, Keegan duct-taped the pipes vertically to a post and trash can, exactly measuring the spread to six feet. We measured again and put on safety glasses.

Prepared with an assortment of small dumbbells ranging from one to three pounds, I also brought along an assortment of box-end wrenches weighed and labeled in two-ounce increments. I positioned myself next to the tank, midway between the poles. Keegan stood to one side where he could see both me and the poles. No harsh noise of the leaf blower, only the soft hissing sound of helium. The tug upward soon became pronounced. I held down the neck of the balloon with one hand while maintaining a tight fit on the nozzle with the other.

"That's it, Papa! You're touching both poles."

"Grab those big rubber bands to tie this thing off! Hold it tight so it can't get away!" I tied weights to the balloon. At five pounds, I added the assorted small wrenches until we reached neutral buoyancy.

"Five pounds, four ounces, that's what a six-foot balloon will lift! Now stand back while I ease out the helium."

I can do it! Just like in my dreams. I'm going to make my grandkids fly. I ordered six more balloons: two reds, two blues, one yellow, and one green.

On a summer day, I reserved three tanks of helium. All week I monitored the weather forecast for Saturday. Moving fronts and projected wind conditions were critical. I couldn't manage even one of the large balloons with any wind over five miles per hour. On Thursday afternoon, the party store manager muscled three heavy tanks of helium into Mary's SUV. Too heavy to load and unload, I left them in her car. For the next two days, I fretted about Mary being in a wreck with those bombs on board. Friday night, I monitored TV weather channels, radio stations, and aviation weather recordings. All agreed on the forecast: clear sky, light breeze through the morning, wind picking up in the afternoon, five to ten miles per hour.

Tulsa has a spacious open area, Johnson Park, designed without trees or electrical lines for sports. On Saturday morning we had the park all to ourselves. Mary agreed to be our official photographer, to document what went right or wrong. We brought a ribbon tied on a stick to give an index of wind speed and direction.

I addressed the grandkids. "You have all weighed in and know Grant is the only one light enough for the balloons to lift. We have seven balloons to fill. Lauren and Jack will assist me with wrestling tanks out of the car and begin filling balloons. Keegan, place the PVC poles in the ground six feet apart, like we practiced, then unload and spread the dumbbells to temporarily anchor the balloons on the ground."

The first balloon hissed, then hummed.

"It's full, Papa," Lauren shouted. "The balloon is touching each pole."

"Keegan, begin putting Grant into the harness, and bring him over here. We're almost ready with the first one."

We turned off the tank, tied the mouth of the balloon with large rubber bands, and clipped our first proud product to the harness on Grant. Our original plan was to anchor all balloons to dumbbells, then attach them to Grant one at a time, but we were too enthused to follow the plan. Although the massive red balloon lifted only five pounds and a few ounces, our excitement increased when we saw the tug on Grant's harness.

One at a time the grandkids' faces broadened into grins as they saw this was going to work. They began to talk fast and yell. Like an excited puppy, Keegan broke into a run, back and forth, back and forth. Grant, with the balloon tethered to him, tried to join Keegan in a run, but discovered he couldn't run with the wind resistance on the huge balloon. He could only make slow steps by leaning forward against the drag.

"Hold it, Grant. Stop! Walk over here where we can disconnect you for now."

Colorful helium balloons anchored by dumbbells made the park look like a Willy-Wonka playground of giant lollypops. The kids' recklessness escalated with enthusiasm, and the risk of losing a helium-filled balloon increased. If only one balloon pulled free through our fingers, my dream would end because we needed the lifting power of all seven. I was an anxious coach wanting to temper their excitement to keep them focused, but it would have been easier to put socks on a rooster. Meanwhile, I had my own exhilaration to restrain.

Kevin showed up and helped us put a lid on the kids. He quickly understood how to secure the balloons without killing enthusiasm. Mary was busy capturing the chaos on camera.

While we worked feverishly, Grant wandered through us wearing his harness. He carried no fear, just a big grin. He stood by the first dumbbell as we untied the lightweight, fifty-pound test kite string and transferred the balloon to his harness. We walked him to the next dumbbell, repeating the process until all balloons were transferred to the harness, strings cut at different lengths to stagger height and not crowd the balloons. With each attachment, Kevin lifted Grant to test his decreasing weight and my heart rate increased. I had invested over fifty years in this one day and had earned the right to be the most excited.

Seven massive balloons dominated the skyline.

How many grandfathers dream of tying helium balloons to their grandkid and watching that kid slip away forever into a blue sky? In my nightmares the safety line slithers through my fingers, and I watch Grant float away, all because he wants to please me. Unable to yell instructions, the family turns on me with that what-are-you-going-to-do-now look? On the evening news, I am asked to explain my actions to the world. I break through these terrifying nightmares by waking up in a cold sweat.

I rehearsed the numbers over and over in my head. If each balloon lifted five-and-a-half pounds, the total could lift thirty-eight-and-a-half pounds. Grant weighed in that morning at forty-nine pounds. Therefore, he carried a positive weight of ten, enough to prevent him from drifting away. When Kevin lifted Grant to shoulder level and released him, Grant drifted to the ground. Three times we went through the exercise.

A light breeze moved the ribbon tied to a pole.

Lauren fetched the safety line I attached to Grant's harness, not to hold him down, but to protect him in case a wind gust tried to drag him. She would assist him in walking back into the wind. Otherwise, once drifted downwind, walking back into the wind would be like walking upstream in neck-deep water.

Everyone yelled at the same time. "Jump, Grant! Run, Grant! Run and jump, Grant."

Walking as she looked through the camera viewfinder, Mary caught the fever. "Do it, Grant! Jump!"

I took all preparations seriously and had a back-up plan: a pellet rifle to instantly destroy one balloon if seven had too much lift or drag. A gentle breeze tugged at the colorful mass overhead and Grant took upon himself to walk with the wind which pulled him along. He jumped forward six feet and stumbled. Jack and Lauren lifted the fallen gladiator back to his feet.

"Come on, Grant, you know what to do. Go for it!" I hollered.

The balloons pulled on my imaginary harness as I struggled to leap for him. I held my breath as I rolled my shoulders forward, bent at the hips and crouched toward the ground. I pushed against the ground and stood on my toes trying to help him. My heart carried him through the air.

Filled with anticipation and excitement, Jack and Lauren walked on each side of him. Both barked instructions on the sidelines. "Jump, Grant, jump!" Wind continued to push him along as Grant found his rhythm and jumped eight feet, then ten and twelve, beautiful weightless jumps like astronauts on the moon, exactly as I imagined. My dream of a slow back flip was not up to reality, but if I could get Grant to take a giant moon-step, that would be close enough. All three moved in unison across the park while Grant jumped and Jack ran along with his safety line. The rest of us fell in behind screaming and yelling. "That's far enough. Stay away from the trees. Bring him back."

Each of Grant's runs downwind became more fluid with fewer stumbles and smoother jumps. Kevin had an idea. "Grant, since you don't weigh much, I'm going to throw you straight up and let the wind carry you. Okay?" Grant grinned widely.

On the first toss, Kevin threw him at least twenty feet up into the air. Grant squealed with delight as he flew and drifted twenty-five feet downwind to a soft, slow-motion landing. Kevin threw Grant higher and higher until he reached thirty-five feet, the length of the safety line.

Grant was all grins, but a hush fell over us mortals left grounded. Before he reached his peak, Grant's ascension rate slowed. He appeared to hang in the air before drifting down in slow motion against the blue cloudless sky. "Do it again!" Grant pleaded. I took my turn throwing him. No bells, no band, no music accompanied the event, only the sound of distant traffic.

Two generations after my dreams of flying, Grant was the flyer who lingered in the air, slowly drifted down and gracefully landed on a green lawn. Reality proved better than a dream because we were all awake and sharing in a family experience. I smelled the comforting aroma of childhood clouds and touched the sky, the wind washed my heart, my spirit waltzed through the air, and I was thirteen again.

"Papa, are you okay?" Jack asked.

"Never better," I said, turning to hide the moisture in my eyes.

Grant Flying High Above Jack

Lewis & Clark

With small teeth, the travel bug chewed on me. The possibilities of free adventures on an isolated river could perhaps be a new tool in my grandfather bag. Why not borrow a canoe and float down the Arkansas River with a couple of grandkids for a day?

Six Excited Kids — Summer 2007

Maybe a couple of us can canoe all the way from Tulsa to Bixby. I approached my daughters with the proposed adventure two weeks in advance.

"If you're going to take my kids, I want to go," Lori said.

"If Lori's going with her kids, I want to go with my three," Amy said.

Intended to be an easy river float, now all of a sudden I was an expedition leader in charge of equipment and supplies, and the safety of nine souls.

A family friend owned a canoe I was welcome to borrow, but now we needed three more canoes to carry the group. I called the Boy Scouts and learned canoe rental was restricted to members only. I called boat stores and learned they sold canoes and were not in the business to rent. I placed "want to rent" ads on Craigslist and in the local newspaper. Responses confirmed my suspicion that many people purchase canoes with plans for summer fun, use them once or twice, then store them behind a garage to suffer decay and decomposition by nature. The purchase of canoes for fishing and fun ranks up there with New Year's exercise resolutions.

When answering ads in person, I dragged along Lauren, Keegan, and Jack for props. Eager, innocent-looking kids standing next to Granddad add a legitimate air to any negotiation. When I informed owners of my intention to use canoes on the Arkansas River with my

189

daughters and grandkids, two of three turned down my offer to rent and lent me canoes instead with my promise to pay for any damages. All three owners enthusiastically supplied paddles and life jackets, but not one understood why I wanted to paddle down the Arkansas. "Nobody does that," they all told me.

The week before we eased the canoes down the steep riverbank, I worried about managing the logistics of four canoes and nine free spirits without appearing bossy. To my surprise, river access for launching and retrieving boats was limited, a fact I confirmed with close-up satellite images of the banks. Sand-dredging operations offered the most common accesses to water but were spread ten to fourteen miles apart. Few people use the river for fishing, even fewer for recreation. I checked the library for maps of the river and found none. AAA Travel Services and local guide books ignored a river route. I stood on the banks at 41st and 91st Streets to check out our limited access via the park in Tulsa and a sand-dredging outfit down-river south of Jenks. Our trip was unknown to all; Columbus and I were kindred spirits. I promptly resigned myself to working with what I had.

The night before our adventure we gathered the canoes and hid them behind our house in case anyone showed too much interest and pinched them. Packing up sandwiches and junk food, bottles of water, and plenty of sunscreen, we prepared a borrowed trailer and the rack on our SUV.

In the morning we hauled four canoes to the river's edge at the park at 41st Street and Riverside Drive, four blocks from our house. Mary graciously volunteered to deliver and pick us up. Lori and Amy arrived, each with her three kids. We were already an hour behind schedule.

Six excited kids could not slide the first canoe down a steep bank without losing shoes, brushing through poison ivy, and dropping the cooler, all before reaching the water. The cracked Styrofoam cooler leaked in the canoe the rest of our trip. Although the water reached bank to bank with scattered sandbars, the kids could wade through most of the Arkansas River.

Once underway I used a hand-held GPS to measure the river flow rate: two miles per hour. When we all paddled as fast as possible, for less than two minutes, we bumped our speed up to five miles per hour but averaged about three. Three adults and six kids had nine different opinions regarding when, where, and why we stopped or continued. At a leisurely pace we stopped to explore sandbar islands with trees, look for arrowheads, and examine fish skeletons.

Impressed by the lack of billboards, cars, and people, we were simply a traveling family divided into four canoes. I would not have been surprised to see deer at the water's edge. Only a streak of silver dragging its contrails flew across a blue sky. Tens of thousands of people carried on lives beyond the river's banks, but we drifted in isolation. Unlike the touristy Illinois River an hour away, filled with canoes, kayaks, and rafts bumping into one another, drunken yells and loud music, our Arkansas River was silent.

One by one, we stopped talking. When on shore I gaze at the river, but when on the river, I watch the shoreline. Like wayfarers from the past, we stared at the shore as though we were on a mission of discovery.

At one in the afternoon, we passed Jenks and turned east ninety degrees around a long bend into a headwind. Despite the pushing current and our rigorous paddling, we could not overcome the wind. Resting was out of the question because the wind would blow us backwards.

"Daddy, our boat gives up," Lori announced from her canoe.

"Yeah, let's call Mom to pick us up," Amy said.

On the river only half a day! I was not ready to quit. I wanted to see around the river's next bend but knew when I'd been overridden. We pulled into an abandoned sand-dredging operation with a road to the river and called Mary.

Later that evening, I recounted our family river adventure over a glass of wine with my best friend, John Carletti. He told me he wanted to take his grandson and float with us the next summer. I considered turning him down because of my still-fresh experience of having too many people and canoes to coordinate, not to mention the fact that I had no idea whether Carletti possessed any experience paddling a canoe. "Sure, John. Sounds like a plan," I said. "Just you and me and our two grandkids."

Too Many Logistics — Summer 2008

The river's isolation from nearby trappings of civilization dominated my thoughts, expanding into possibilities and numbers. If we traveled seven miles in five hours, counting stops, what was the possibility of canoeing downriver an additional sixty to seventy more miles to Muskogee where I grew up? Perhaps the logistics could be managed with only one canoe and two or three paddlers over several one-day legs.

I counted on Mary's willingness to drop us off where we ended last year's leg and pick us up downriver. Now I needed to recruit one or two grandkids. I excluded the twins, busy with high school commitments and no longer interested in traveling with mothers and grandfather. I did, however, expect the other four grandkids to be willing members of the crew.

Lauren brushed her stylish hair off her shoulders. "Thanks for the invite, Papa, but I got paddling out of my system last year."

Jack was a seasoned Scout who would know how to spend the night along the river if we wanted to. And I wanted to. He looked at his feet. "No thanks, Papa, I have Scout camp that weekend."

Keegan juggled his soccer ball. "Papa, I have soccer practice. I want to make the team."

My great adventure hung on eight-year-old Grant. "Grant, would you paddle a canoe down the river with me? Nana will drop us off where we got out last year and we'll paddle and play until we find a place where we want to get out and call her." He agreed, apparently with unconditional faith in my judgment, knowing I would never place him in harm's way.

With one grandkid committed to canoeing, I entered the seductive world of planning an adventure. Grant saw the trip as going somewhere and doing something with me, but I envisioned a more grandiose plan. I craved more details: topographic maps, aerial maps, satellite images, and river history. I saw to it that he understood the river geography and history, including early exploration of the Great Plains and settlements by the Five Civilized Tribes following the Trail of Tears. I watched the website, "River Flow Rate in Oklahoma," to determine adequate flow and safety. Based on the distance we traveled on this second leg, I could estimate how many more years would be required to complete my grand expedition.

Ten days before our scheduled trip, Carletti heard about my plans and called to remind me that he and his grandson wanted to join us. I figured another kid would make the trip more fun for Grant. John and I could paddle one borrowed canoe with our grandsons sitting in the middle on either side of a cooler.

Too many logistics. Too many personalities. Two hours behind our projected schedule, Mary dropped the four of us off in the midmorning sun by the sand-dredging operation where our family had exited the river last year. John and I carried our canoe down to the river on the access road.

The boys matched well at eight years old and sixty pounds each in the center of the canoe. John held the canoe while I sat my 170 pounds down in the bow position and John, a happy upbeat Italian, weighed down the stern at 230 pounds.

What was I thinking? I tried to scoot the cooler toward the front with me, but a cross bar foiled my attempted weight adjustment. The boys decided the cooler made a great perch. Rationalizing we had invested too much effort to cancel our trip, I waved goodbye to Mary as John pushed us away from the shore.

All I could locate before the trip for the boys to use as paddles was one small paddle and a child's plastic shovel. Neither of them accepted the shovel as a real paddle, so I had them switch every ten minutes so neither would feel slighted. From their positions high atop the cooler, however, they could not effectively paddle or steer and soon lost interest, reverting to simply splashing the paddle and shovel.

Within the first half hour, we approached a narrow strait as wide as the canoe was long but only six inches deep. The flow rate suddenly picked up. Our unbalanced canoe and uncoordinated paddling caused us to enter the strait sideways instead of lining up to pass down a small rapids through the choke point. The front end of the canoe lodged on the left shore and the back wedged against the right. Water pressure built on the upstream side and turned the canoe over in slow motion.

Crew and supplies flopped and emptied themselves into the shallow swift water. Three of us struggled to gain a foothold while cooler lid, goods, and the small paddle washed downstream. We salvaged the Styrofoam cooler to keep it from polluting the river, found an unfazed Grant in a pocket of air under the canoe, lost my Swiss Army knife, the shovel and our sandwiches, but to the kids' delight, we recovered our junk food.

"Was that our morning entertainment?" John asked, peering out from under his crooked hat.

The kids ran around splashing in the shallow water; no one was hurt or upset. Gathering ourselves and remaining supplies into the canoe, we accepted the event as a challenge that went along with our uncharted water journey. My intuition had been trying to tell me that one canoe is best handled by two paddlers of relatively equal weight. Progress was painfully slow for the next three hours. We stopped to wander across sandbars to pee, eat junk food for lunch, and let the kids run around.

Two years in a row I felt disappointed with our progress. I grinned at Grant when we found ourselves alone on a sandbar. "Thanks for being a good sport to take others with us, but next year it will be just you and me. At this rate I'm not going to live long enough to finish my grand plan." I took my cell phone out of its three plastic bags and called Mary.

"How's it going?" she asked.

"I don't even want to talk about it."

In four hours of scorching sun, we traveled only seven miles, climbing out of the water one mile downriver from Highway 64 near Bixby. The four of us carried our canoe up the weedy bank to the parking lot of the Indian Springs soccer complex. Mary stood waiting for us.

Ridding the River of Bad Guys — Summer 2009

Mary drove nine-year-old Grant and me to the soccer field overlooking the river's edge where we stopped the prior July. By now he had grown enough that the two of us could successfully load and unload the borrowed canoe from the car roof and drag it through the slippery grass, easing it down the high bank on a rope.

According to the website, river flow was up, but the increased volume could not be appreciated because the water spread from bank to bank, measuring only one to three feet deep with our paddles. A specific map of the river had never been printed, so we used a AAA highway map with a thin blue line representing the river. No details. Unable to see past the riverbanks, we oriented our position by time and bridges. The GPS gave us speed only, longitude and latitude being worthless on the river.

Preparations included launching on time at sunup with a cooler of sandwiches, apples, bananas, eight bottles of water, two cold beers for me. We also brought along a BB gun for Grant. Mary sent more sunscreen than drinking water. Grant and I needed it because we could be poster boys for the term "paleface." Towheaded Grant looked like he had a perpetual suntan compared to me; I looked like a glass of milk. I burn easily and apply so much lotion that Lori often says I look like the icing on a Dolly Madison cupcake. Grant and I wore large-brimmed hats that could blow us upstream if the wind picked up.

For the first time pushing into the river, we were but two. Not a cloud in the sky, not a breeze, just two congenial souls paddling one canoe. When we sweated, the sunscreen washed down our bodies onto the canoe's aluminum seats. Normally when we pulled on a stroke, we sat firm in our seats. But with the sunscreen-slicked seats, we slid forward with each stroke.

"Let's pull over into the shallows and wipe down our seats," I said.

"Papa, I bumped over a bottle of lotion and stepped on it. I'll need to wipe it up. The bottom of the canoe is too slick to stand up."

Lewis and Clark never faced this problem.

Daybreak gave way to midmorning as we settled in on a casual speed and rhythm. Grant had never been around a BB gun, so I gave him instructions on how to point and shoot the Red Ryder I brought. I helped him practice cocking the gun without ever leaving the lever open. He assumed guardianship of our boat and reinforced our safety from river pirates with his personal weapon. From the bow he was free to aim and shoot any direction except behind him.

Just me and my grandson floating and paddling down that lazy river. No hurry. No particular destination. I steadied the canoe, pointing downstream past the Conjada Mountains and Stone Bluff, while he slew river dragons, pinged floating sticks, and popped the water's edge. Visits alternated with silence. No television, telephone, cell phone, other personalities, agendas, schedules, places to be. No competition on the river.

"Papa?" Grant said as he turned to face me, resting his paddle across his lap. "When I have children, I want to do this with them. Will you come with us?"

"Sure. I'd like that." My heart soared. He turned back and began his long easy strokes. I hugged myself trying to contain my joy.

I matched his easy whish, whish, whish rhythm that did not fatigue. He developed a pattern of recognizable strokes like a man develops his individual walk. My grandson's graceful strokes inspired me to wonder if my granddaddy or daddy had ever considered taking me down this same river. If so, we could have a tradition.

For the first time, Grant was a prime member of our crew. Grandfather and grandson connected in adventure and wordless communion. His ability to anticipate and make paddling adjustments impressed me. If only the two of us had been in the canoe last summer, we would have steered correctly and not turned over. I convinced myself that Grant and I could have held our own as crew members with Lewis and Clark.

When Grant tired of ridding the river of bad guys and water dragons with the BB gun, I wanted to prolong the novelty of the open space. "See how straight up you can shoot and get a BB to land next to us," I said.

Grant turned with a furrowed brow. "It won't come down and hurt us?"

"No problem. We're wearing big-brimmed hats. Trust me. We did this when I was a kid. A falling BB won't hurt us, especially with our hats. Before you shoot, lay your paddle across your knees to protect your exposed skin. After you shoot, lay your gun down, sit straight and keep your hands next to your chest to protect them under your hat."

"Can I tell my parents we did this?"

"Let's just keep it to ourselves. Parents may not understand if they're not here." In fact, they might not let him come with me next year.

Playing the wind with straight-up shots, the closest he came to the canoe with a BB was one that plinked the water on the left side near me. When the novelty of trying to shoot ourselves passed, we settled in for more solitude, an occasional stroke to align the canoe with the current. Far down the river a large gaggle of Canada geese were feeding in shallow water directly in our path. "Grant," I whispered, "move slow, put your paddle in the boat, and lie down in the boat. I'm doing the same." He was small enough to fit on his back, full length, with his feet under his seat. My legs stretched out on each side of the cooler. "Don't raise your head to look or you'll scare 'em. Stay on your back and look straight up. We'll see how close we can get."

"Papa, I'm lying in warm water and sunscreen lotion down here," he snickered.

"Shhh. I am, too, but it'll be worth it."

We drifted into the middle of the gaggle. Geese closest to the canoe lifted off the water to fly over us. Five treated us like a log and flew low and slow directly across, so close we felt their silent wings pressing down on the air with each stroke. Well past the gaggle, we remained quiet in the bottom of the canoe digesting the drama of being that close to wildlife. Watching occasional clouds in a trance, we continued on our backs drifting and bumping along the edge of a sandbar.

In late afternoon, we turned a bend south of Coweta and the edge of a bridge came into view far down the river. Highway 104 crossed the river to Haskell and was the only potential exit where Mary could pick us up. I called her with an estimated time to the bridge of at least an hour.

Scanning the steep bank for the smoothest spot to exit so we could drag the canoe through the weeds up to the road to meet Mary, we encountered the first other person of the day, a lone fisherman sitting on a cooler in a cove with a fishing rod. The only logical place to leave the river was next to him. Fortunately, his fishing line entered the water on our left, and we steered toward him on the downriver side of his line. Would he be friendly or hostile when we invaded his fishing spot?

He watched us steer toward him. "Where you come from? I seen you comin' way up there." He remained seated on a cooler, gripping a fishing rod in his right hand and holding both a cigarette and a beer in his left. Between gulps of beer, he twisted his hand for a drag from his cigarette, never spilling a drop of beer. Years of practice were evident. A prominent mole grew in the crevice between his cheek and nose.

"Bixby," I said, wondering how he could reel in a catch with both hands full.

"You mean to tell me a kid and an old man paddled all the way from Bixby?" He shook his head in disbelief. Or maybe it was more in dismay that the two of us had so thoughtlessly disturbed his waters and scared away the fish.

"I don't know about an old man," I said, grinning and tilting my head toward Grant, "but me and this kid here paddled the Arkansas River from Bixby this morning."

Pushing up the front of an old western hat with a tired feather hanging off the back, he dragged the side of his hand and index finger across his cigarette-stained mustache. He stood and rocked back and forth on his heels, raising his chin and stretching his neck to look upstream over the trees toward Bixby.

"Well, I'll be," he said, grinding out his cigarette with his boot. "Let me help you and the kid. Kinda boring 'round here today. Fish ain't good, and my beer's empty."

Mary shook her head when we climbed up to meet her. After the fisherman left, she asked, "Where'd you pick him up?"

"On a sandbar under the bridge. Couldn't get Grant to keep paddling and I needed help."

"Right, Harold."

The River Less Traveled — Summer 2010

At sunup on a scorching end-of-July day, Mary delivered Grant and me with our canoe and supplies to the bridge near Haskell. Now ten years old, Grant graduated to a medium-length paddle. Now seventy-three years old, I smartened up enough to swallow a dose of Celebrex before leaving home.

Grant pulled a stroke longer and faster than I could. With pride, I watched my lean and sinewy grandson outperform me. Sometimes we switched places in the canoe while I sat in the bow and he practiced steering from the stern. According to our AAA highway map, a train-track bridge waited around the next bend at Yahola Siding. "Papa," Grant said, pointing ahead, "there's that bridge where we can get some shade."

With the canoe pulled ashore, we ate a leisurely lunch and pressed ourselves to drink more water. We relished our moments sitting on the gentle slope under the bridge and looked for excuses to linger against an abutment. A low rumble in the distance.

"Hear that?" Grant asked. I nodded, trying to identify what I couldn't really hear. "It's a train coming, Papa. Do we need to get out of here?"

"No, we're okay." I patted him on his knee. "I've never been under a bridge when a train rumbled over. Let's lie down right here. This could be exciting."

We stared at the empty tracks overhead. Vibrations shuddered through our bodies with increasing intensity as the train approached, the roar reaching us before we saw the train. I motioned to Grant to lie down next to me. On our backs with palms down and fingers splayed on the dirt, we felt every vibration. Wheels and bellies of train cars passed over no more than fifteen feet above us with a deafening clickity-clack, clickity-clack. Concerned about the relentless vibration, Grant stood and walked down to the river and pulled the canoe higher on shore.

The train overhead made noise that would shame a jet. We lost count after sixty-two cars, estimating over one hundred. Unable to talk or yell over the racket, we converted to hand motions when we could tolerate taking our hands off our ears. When sound faded into the distance, we sat up in the lingering odors of diesel fumes, hot wheels, and mysterious cargo.

Grant grinned at me. "We don't have to do that again, do we?"

"No. Once is enough." My ears still ringing, I reached for a beer.

We saw the entrance to the only marina on our journey of discovery, three miles ahead into the wind. The water had cleared after merging with the Grand River below Ft. Gibson Lake. For the first time, we could see the ends of our paddles pulling through water.

Although Grant sat in the bow, I sensed he felt the rhythm of our strokes. Without a drumbeat, background music, or counting aloud, our paddles reached up and forward in concert, preparing to take

a bite of water before plunging in rhythmic sync. Again and again
we pulled, lifted our paddles out of the water simultaneously, and
brought them forward as though we were joined by an invisible force.
I imagined we looked like the wheels of a train engine with a steel bar
linking the driving wheels. We were linked, too, by shared purpose
and intuition. Our journey was more valuable than the destination. I
didn't want the love and comfort of our grandfather-grandson connection to end.

Here we were near the town I grew up in, the town from which
my daddy took the family on Sunday drives back to his childhood
on the Illinois River. After ten hours on the river, we pulled into the
marina. On the launching ramp, Mary stood with Lauren beside her,
both grinning and waving excitedly.

My Dry River — Summer 2011

The clear and cold Arkansas River headwater, fueled by melted
snow, begins as a rivulet on the eastern slope of the Rocky Mountains
west of Leadville, Colorado, ten miles east of the Continental Divide.
Hundreds of miles of rushing waters scour sandstone, draining topsoil
across the eastern plains of Colorado, Kansas, and Oklahoma. Multiple dams create lakes and reservoirs of still water, but water roaring
out of the gates churns up sand, delivering limited clarity downriver.

Lack of rainfall throughout 2011 starved lakes and rivers in the
Southwest, affecting the Missouri and Arkansas drainage basins

Standing in the park at 41st Street and Riverside in the company
of eleven-year-old Grant and sixteen-year-old Jack, I looked out
across the Arkansas, my mind drifting back in time, the kids waiting
for the story they knew was imminent. Feeling like my daddy on the
banks of the Illinois, I paused to collect memories.

"Four years ago, Grant and I began our long canoe trip, but today
the river is low enough to walk across."

"Never heard of walking across a river," Jack said.

"I walked across with your mothers when they were kids and it
was this low. Didn't get our ankles wet." I pointed upriver just below

the Zink low-water dam. "That dam hadn't been built yet. I wanted you to see an empty river. After seeing the water from bank to bank year after year, this is weird."

Looking downriver, I started to laugh. "I remember the year Carletti and his grandson paddled with us. Our unbalanced canoe flipped over and out we flopped into the river." Four hands shot up, twenty fingers splayed to tell me they had already heard this story many times. Undeterred, I continued, "Your mothers stood here with me when they were children. Now I get to walk across the dry river with you who may never see this aberration again in your lifetime." I loved being the first to show my kids and grandkids something they would never forget. Made me feel important.

Grant eyed the riverbed. "Is it safe?"

"Sure. We'll be walking on sand, just like on the beach."

"Any quicksand?"

"Naw. That's just in movies," Jack said.

We walked across a sandbar at least one hundred yards wide. Two slow-moving streams meandered around as we headed upstream to the low-water dam. Removing our shoes we waded the shallow warm waters which, at their deepest, wet our ankles. We discussed the drought and hoped never to see the river so low again.

"Maybe I can walk across the river like this with my kids," Jack said.

"Maybe. But I hope not."

"I'd rather be in a canoe," Grant said.

Knowing When to Quit — Summer 2011

I stopped at the park to ponder a dry river, worried there might not be enough water flowing into Keystone Lake for my proposed one-day final leg, from dam to Tulsa where we had begun. At home I checked the river-flow website projections. Keystone Dam, fifteen miles upstream, would soon begin releasing more water. I tested my idea on Jack and Grant.

"Hey, the Internet shows there will be a good flow in the river in a week. Probably last for weeks. The guy who loaned us a canoe the past four summers has sold it, but I have a friend who is a kayak buff. He has three we can borrow. Any interest?"

"Going from where to where and when?" Jack said.

"Keystone Dam to Zink Lake, close to the spot we put in the river four years ago with the family. Fifteen miles. Easy day. I know the kayaks will be available two weeks from Saturday."

"Sorry, I have a camp-out with the Scouts that weekend, Papa," Jack said, shaking his head. "Would like to join you, but I can't make it."

I was disappointed but knew how committed he was to scouting. Soccer commitments eliminated Lauren and Keegan. Max was in New Zealand as an exchange student and Sam held down a job.

"Grant, just you and me. Okay?"

"Okay. But I have to check with Mom."

Even with extensive paddling experience, Grant remained responsible enough to ask permission. I was impressed. I looked forward to floating the final leg with him. Thereafter, we would have earned bragging rights to know we had floated and paddled eighty miles of the Arkansas River from below Keystone Dam to Muskogee. Perhaps in future years I could conjure an excuse to talk another grandkid into canoeing from Muskogee to the Mississippi River. In one-day legs, of course. If I burned out one grandkid, I could always ask another.

In preparation for our journey I decided to take Grant to the Summit Club, a private restaurant offering a panoramic view from the thirty-third floor of the river and surrounding topography. Not a member, only an occasional guest, I thought the best time to avoid patrons and enjoy the view would be ten o'clock in the morning. I advised Grant to dress appropriately: no shorts. Surely management would sympathize with a grandfather and grandson wanting a quick view.

Anxious about getting past the restaurant staff, I rehearsed the anticipated encounter. First I would ask the manager for permission and, like a politician, have Grant stand in front of me with my hands on his shoulders. I would proceed with my story of educating my grandson about the landmarks of our proud city, along with our plans to kayak down the river. I coached Grant to smile while I recounted our four years of river experiences and explained why the purposed trip was an important conclusion to our river journey from Keystone Dam to Muskogee. I was pumped.

Stepping off the elevator, we discovered the restaurant was vacant. We had the whole place to ourselves with no one to hear my rehearsed story. West-facing windows looked over the fifteen-mile stretch of river we were planning to paddle. With the morning sun behind us, we could see almost to the halfway point, the bridge at Sand Springs. Holding a AAA highway map between us, oohing and awing at the view, I pointed out the landmark bridges, buildings, and roads, and matched them with the map.

On the way down in the elevator, I congratulated myself on the thorough orientation I'd given my grandson. Still full of myself, I took Grant to my friend's house to confirm that two kayaks would fit the rack of our SUV. They fit, but the sides of each would hang two inches over the roof. With enough bungee cords I could stabilize the wobbly kayaks on our rack.

The next day, I searched the Internet and purchased fifty feet of continuous bungee cord. My order also included one hundred hooks necessary for tying on the cut cord. For two nights, I sat through National Geographic documentaries, cutting the cord to varying lengths and applying the hooks.

The following week, I watched the river flow rate, which remained steady and safe. The weather forecast was equally good: light and variable southwestern winds in the morning picking up in the afternoon. As our planned segment of the river flowed straight east, light winds would provide us with a small tailwind boost.

The evening before our departure, Grant and I loaded the two kayaks on top of the SUV. With great care, we balanced them and began securing them with the bungee cords. While I connected one side to the body frame underneath the car, Grant hooked under the opposite side to produce balanced pull. We followed the same pattern with the front and back by crisscrossing the remaining cords to compensate for side winds. By the time we ran out of bungee cords, we counted twenty-three, a sure sign of amateur overkill. The SUV looked like it had a giant spider web covering the kayaks from bumper to bumper, affecting my ability to see out the front and back windshields while driving home.

I monitored the flow rate one more time before going to bed, awakened at 5:00 a.m., long before my alarm went off, and raced to my computer to confirm the flow rate had not changed. Good. No surprises. We could launch our boats by about eight in the morning. Paddling at the conservative speed of one mile per hour, and with the current carrying us along at two miles per hour, I estimated five hours on the water. We needed to budget time to explore, visit, and tell each other how smart we were.

With ever-faithful Mary along as our support crew, I picked up Grant and his mother, Amy, a little before seven. We arrived below the dam at 8:00 a.m. sharp. Contrary to my usual detailed planning, I had not accurately measured the distance of our trip route. Using the highway map, the only map available, I estimated a distance of fifteen miles. To my surprise that morning, my odometer measured nineteen miles, a world of difference when one is paddling.

Unable to find a launching site, we stopped in a parking lot below Keystone Dam and stared at the river. "Where's the water?" I said, startled that no water flowed from the massive dam. I could not accept what I saw. While others released bungee cords, I remained fixated on the river. It looked naked without fast-flowing water from bank to bank. Residual shallow pools covered the river bottom with scant water flowing downstream between them. Having invested so much time and energy into this trip, I rationalized the remaining river volume to be sufficient to carry a single person in a shallow draft kayak. The flow had obviously been shut down within the previous three hours. A passing uncertainty bumped the side of my head. For a moment, I debated whether my decision was wishful thinking or reality. To stop now would require reloading the kayaks, returning them, waiting for another good weather report, and coordinating our schedules. I pushed reality behind me. To my way of thinking, if we paddled fast enough at the upper end of low water, we could catch up to the larger downstream body and coast with the stream.

Grant and I slipped and stumbled and dragged the kayaks down the rocky forty-foot-high bank. When we looked back up, it looked at least eighty-feet high, far too high to drag the kayaks back uphill and reload.

Grant tilted his head back far enough to see under the wide brim of his hat, waiting for me to make a decision. Mary and Amy stood at the top of the high bank also waiting to see what action I was going to take.

"I think we should go for it," I said.

"Okay, Papa," Grant said without hesitation or questioning my judgment

Yelling our intentions to Mary and Amy, I pointed to my chest, then at Grant and pointed downstream. I repeated the plan by bending my arm ninety degrees at my elbow then straightening it out to point downstream.

Mary and Amy mouthed inaudible words and waved goodbye before disappearing from sight. At last we launched the kayaks and headed downriver. Between the current and paddling, I believed we could coast, paddle, and visit.

Rocks ranging in size from softballs to refrigerators covered the river bottom. Water spewing from the gates had blasted away lightweight sand for miles. Remaining water flowed from one pool to another over a series of rapids dropped six feet over a distance of thirty. The kayaks dragged against the large rocks, but rushing water and our pushing against the river bottom with paddles helped us navigate the first rapids.

At the end of the third pool, which favored the left bank, we were surprised not to find an outlet. Mystified, we pulled to the bank, stood on a log and discovered a large long pool near the opposite bank with no connecting open water. The water seeped through the sand from one pool to the other. Our only option was to drag our kayaks across two hundred yards of sand to the next body of water. The next two half-mile strips of water presented the same obstacle. Although we stopped often to eat and replenish our fluids, I began to fatigue. Grant showed no signs of tiring.

Entering the next large pool, we picked up a headwind of five miles per hour. Without a current, we needed to paddle harder to overcome the wind. Paddling side-by-side was no longer viable; in the headwind, we traveled with one kayak drafting the one behind.

When the headwind died, I pulled ahead fifty feet and my skinny butt screamed for a change of position. I couldn't shift left or right, forward or backward. My only option was to push up and rest behind my seat. I figured after a few minutes of change my butt would recover. A kayak's stability, however, relies on distribution of weight as close to the bottom as practical. One's butt rests on a thin cushion, about two inches from the bottom. Breaking a cardinal rule for a kayak, "always sit in the seat at the bottom," I pushed myself up with both arms and sat behind the seat.

The kayak didn't turn over, it flipped over faster than a light switch. I didn't have time to yell before popping up beside the kayak holding my hat and sunglasses. Before I could orient myself to the nearest bank, Grant saw me in the water with the kayak upside-down, closed the distance and came alongside. "Papa, hold onto the back of my kayak, I'll pull us to shore."

He paddled and dragged me while I hung onto the rear of his kayak with one hand and towed my upside-down vessel with the other. We needed to pull ashore to dump water and resume paddling from a stable position. I was trying to swim with a long-sleeved light-weight sun-blocking shirt and pants. Kicking to help Grant, I lost a shoe. Food, water, and a dry change of clothes were protected in a watertight compartment, but not an extra pair of shoes. Normally, we wore our life vests at all times, except when the water was calm and jackets chafed our armpits when we paddled, which was our present condition.

I crawled out of the water on rocks, flopped over on my back, spread my arms and legs wide, gasped for air, and stared at the sky.

"Papa, are you okay?"

"Yeah," I said between breaths. "Tough swimming in a long-sleeved shirt, pants, and one shoe."

He never passed judgment on me or asked why I turned over in my kayak, almost as if this were an unsurprising event for his grandfather. Even though we were two guys on the river, my responsibility was to watch out for him. I mentally flogged myself.

Into the third hour of an estimated five-hour trip, we used a radio tower as a landmark and discovered we had navigated only four of the nineteen miles. The already-limited river water continued to drain from under us, as we lost time righting the kayak on the bank. We gobbled a sandwich and pushed off chewing.

On our canoe trips over the years, I always packed gloves but never used them. This time I found I had packed two left gloves. We were up that proverbial creek, only we had paddles, but our hands were too blistered to use them. I gave both left gloves to Grant. He used one backward on his right hand. I removed my once-white socks that looked like they strained muck, and wore them loosely over my hands so I could hold a paddle.

We approached the end of a mile-long pool where the water emptied down a thirty-foot slope of gravel and sand. As the day progressed, lifting myself out of the kayak became more difficult. Instead of getting out and dragging the boat over the small rapids, I elected to push myself with my paddle, bumping along in the shallows. I added negligible force by throwing my head and shoulders forward trying to scoot. Less than halfway down a long rapids, I could not move despite rocking and pushing with my paddle. Much lighter, Grant scooted around me in his kayak and descended into the next pool. He climbed out, dragged his kayak away from the rushing water, and waded upstream to me. Gathering the rope from my bow, he began pulling me down the shallow rapids.

"Grant," I said, waving my paddle, "you shouldn't pull me. I'll get out and walk."

"Papa, you've pulled and lifted me for the last four years. I'm big enough to help you now. Please, just sit." He leaned back and carefully dragged me over the shallows. I was limited in helping but unlimited in being impressed.

Farther downriver, small rocks disappeared leaving a familiar sandy river bottom. As the water level dropped, we began seeing more sand and less water. Sometimes we paddled to the end of a pool only to see the water reappear hundreds of yards further downstream.

"There's the Sand Springs Bridge up ahead, about a mile," I said, pointing with my paddle. "Halfway point."

With heads down like mules, we waded and pulled our kayaks over sand and one-inch strips of water. By now we wore our life jackets as horse collars to pad our shoulders from the ropes attached to the bow of our kayaks.

"What time is it?" Grant asked.

"Ten after four."

"We've been on the river over six hours and aren't halfway yet. It's going to be dark by the time we get there." Grant paused as though giving me time to digest the statement. "I don't think we should be out here after dark, but I'll stay with you as long as you like."

Thinking his logic over, I retrieved my cell phone from the kayak's watertight compartment and peeled off three Ziploc bags. "Mary, can you pick us up at the soccer field by the north side of the Sand Springs Bridge?" I wondered if she heard the defeat in my voice.

Grant arrived on shore first, dragged his kayak to safety and waded out to me. While I remained seated, he pulled the bow as far on shore as possible, straddled the front and held each side to prevent rocking as I lifted myself out. Walking my hands up my thighs, I stood up in increments, tottered out of the water and up the bank, squatted and dropped the rest of the way into a sitting position. "Ugh!" I grunted, drawing in long deep breaths while Grant gathered up our supplies.

After spending months planning the trip, I could not comprehend the thought of not completing the final leg. I was responsible for logistics and safety on the trip, but, of the two of us, my eleven-year-old grandson displayed the maturity of knowing when to quit and said so with diplomacy. My pride for him outstripped my embarrassment at not knowing when to quit. I just might not tell Mary which one of us was wise enough to stop.

Skinny Three-Foot Gars — Summer 2012

Before Grant and I pushed off into the Arkansas River from the soccer field at Sand Springs and Mary and Amy pulled away, I checked my list and confirmed that along with food, water, and sunscreen, we had packed two pairs of gloves, both left and right, strap-on hats, dry toilet paper, and my cell phone in three watertight bags. I wanted to go over the finish line with Grant by my side. Soccer was beginning to dominate his time and that day was the only window of time for me and the river. Turbines had been opened overnight; water was expected to run for a day or two.

Slipping kayaks through weeds to the water's edge, I gave a sigh of relief that the water flowed well. "Grant, you lead. I'll follow or come alongside to visit."

My GPS showed us drifting along at two miles per hour without paddling. After five years and miles of river travel, we saw our first white-tailed deer about two-hundred yards ahead. "Papa," Grant whispered, "don't move or paddle," but the antlered buck was already running away. We had seen perch on earlier trips, but, for the first time, we shared the river with two-foot carp and occasional long and skinny three-foot gars.

Paddling around a bend covered with giant sycamore trees, the downtown skyline of Tulsa stretched across the river. We passed in view of the Summit Club windows. *Coming home.* A right-angled turn headed us south into an unexpected headwind. Paddling hard we focused on the wind.

"Hear that traffic noise?"

"Papa, that's rapids we're hearing," Grant said, paddling beside me.

"That's the last thing I expected to hear or see on this river. What do you think?"

For my benefit, because I knew he wouldn't have any problem shooting the rapids, he said, "I say we walk along the edge and line the boats down until we pass the rapids."

We paused under the construction of the new 11th Street Bridge and paddled into the headwaters of the low-water Zink Dam, past the west River Park where once stood a tantalizing trapeze. Downriver, the Tulsa Rowing Club was practicing with brisk coordinated strokes. Ours may never have been as coordinated, but they steered us into real-life adventures together, grandfather and grandson. Our sixth year on the river. I had never dreamed of tackling a multi-year project.

"Grant!" I hollered, startling him. In high drama, I stepped out of my kayak into eighteen inches of warm water. Removing my hat with my left hand and holding the kayak from drifting away, I scanned the east and west banks. Jamming the paddle with my right hand into the sandy bottom, I shouted, "In the name of Grant King and Harold Battenfield, I hereby claim this run of the Arkansas River from Keystone Dam to Muskogee!"

"We earned it, Papa!"

"For years, I have heard talk of more low-water dams on this river," I said, looking at the back of Grant's head. "If so, you will tell your children about how it used to be open water."

The sixth leg of our river dream gave us bragging rights, but no one cared except the two of us. Our destination was never as important as the process. Over the years Grant's weight had doubled and he grew five inches; my hair grew white and my back tired more quickly. The once untamed and unpredictable Arkansas River continued to swell and dry in accordance with snowmelt in the mountains, crop requirements in the plains, government regulations, and, more recently, dams.

Understanding — Summer 2012

One Sunday when I was seventy-five, I stood beside Grant on the banks of the Arkansas River waving to Mary and Amy in the grass along Riverside Drive. It was then I understood the connection of time to landscape, water to land, dreams to real-life drama. It was then I realized how much like my daddy I was. Even without the full masculine neck and comb-straightened hair, I experienced action-packed adventures of my own and tales to tell. It was then I recognized the magical connection I had yearned for ever since I could remember: my life as one unique strand in a never-ending, comforting braid of generations. Many of my dreams were born as I lay in a cradle of darkness next to Grandma Rosie. The boy lives inside me. His dreams are still mine.

Grant and Jack Almost Dry on the Arkansas River

Harold and Grant on the Arkansas River Below Keystone Dam

Return to Our Home

Three dollars? Six cents per year? By the numbers it didn't look right, but it felt right.

Three dollars bought a slab of sandstone the size of a one-and-a-half-inch-thick table placemat that I would transform into the first of two surprises for Mary on our fiftieth anniversary. After experimenting with design options using pencil and paper, I decided on a big heart with "50 YEARS IN LOVE" in the middle in bold letters. On the left side of the heart was "Mary" and on the right "Harold," not like on a tombstone but as in a declaration. Underneath would scroll "1959-2009." The rock could be leaned upright on the fireplace or used as a garden stepping stone.

I gave myself four months lead time, keeping the rock in the trunk of my car in order to slip in a half hour of chiseling now and then. Before coming home from work, I often sat on a park bench next to the Arkansas River with the sandstone across my lap, safety glasses protecting my eyes. I sculpted with a tack hammer and an engraver's chisel while listening to music of the fifties and sixties on my iPod: Country Western, Broadway musicals, timeless romantic Golden Oldies. Hormones raged in our teens and twenties when Mary and I cut our teeth on those ballads. The strike of my hammer kept rhythm with the beat of the music, tapping out small flakes to the romantic songs of Frank Sinatra. When Elvis sang, my foot tapped with gusto and the chisel drove faster and deeper.

Nearing completion at the end of the third month, I moved the forty-pound sandstone slab from my car trunk and hid it in the garage, leaning it on the dark side of my workbench, away from Mary's eyes. Whenever she took one of the grandkids on an errand or went grocery shopping, they warned me with a text message on the way home. The subterfuge allowed me time to hide my secret, brush chips off my clothes, and grab a yard tool as cover.

∽

Soon it was time to arrange the second surprise for Mary. I made a call. "Joyce, this is Harold Battenfield, your old neighbor." Although she didn't know it, Joyce was an important component of my anniversary plan. "I have a strange favor to ask. Our fiftieth anniversary is coming up, and I want to surprise Mary by visiting our old house. It was a big part of our lives. We created lots of memories there, mostly good, some sad. I need the name and phone number of the person who lives in it now. Is this too crazy?"

"An unusual request but not crazy. You folks always saw the world a little differently than most. I miss that. The owner is a single man, a nice guy named Todd Jackson. I'll get his number while we're on the line. I think he's out of town this weekend, but I'll tell him to expect your call."

Like a salesman before a presentation, I wrote and rehearsed a script so as not to arouse any suspicion about my motive. "Hi. Am I speaking to Todd Jackson?"

"That's me." His voice was firm but pleasant.

"My name is Harold Battenfield." I licked my lips and swallowed. "My family lived in your house forty years ago."

He chuckled. "Joyce told me to expect your call. She wasn't real clear about what you had in mind. Tell me about it."

"We lived in your house for seven years and loved it. A week from Saturday my wife and I celebrate our fiftieth anniversary. I'd like to walk with her and my kids and grandkids through your house for old times' sake. How would 4:00 p.m. work for you?"

"Fine," he said without needing further explanation. "The house will be yours as an anniversary gift. I've already made plans to go next door with Joyce for a cup of coffee."

∽

Friday morning, I woke up early, staring in the dark with a silly grin, planning my next move. I slipped from under the covers, walked around to Mary's side of the bed and sat next to her while she was still asleep. I wanted the visit to be a surprise, but not by springing it on her as we pulled up to the house. Despite my enthusiasm, she might not welcome such a visit because we had never fully processed Beth's death while we lived there. A visit might trigger painful memories for her. I gently shook her shoulder. "Mary, I've got something to tell you."

"Wha … huh?" She was still half asleep.

"I've planned a surprise for you," I said, leaning over next to her ear.

"What've you done now?" she mumbled from under the covers.

"I've made arrangements to tour our old home tomorrow. Remember Joyce and Jim next door?"

She slowly blinked twice, then closed her eyes. "I'm going back to sleep." She rolled her back to me and pulled the covers over her head.

"Wait a minute," I said, leaning closer. "Just listen for a minute."

"Talk fast."

"Well, if you remember, Jim died three years ago, but I called Joyce about the guy who lives in our old house. I needed her as a reference so when I called him he wouldn't think I was casing his house."

"And he said okay?" Mary said from under the covers.

"He and Joyce are caught up in the idea and he sounded genuinely flattered."

While she was getting out of bed, I cooked our routine three-minute oatmeal and brewed the coffee. She found the slab of sandstone resting atop the morning paper on the kitchen table. She slid into her chair, studied it, looked out the kitchen window and back at the slab. "Now *that* is a wonderful surprise. Let me see your hands. How did you do this without cuts or bruises?" She traced her index finger over the engraved heart and letters and kept the rock on the table throughout the day, stopping from time to time to stroke it.

᠀

A limousine arrived on Saturday afternoon, an anniversary gift from our daughters and sons-in-law to chauffeur our three-generation family of twelve. We toured our honeymoon site, the Will Rogers Motel, replaced by a pharmacy. From there we drove past the OSU Medical Center and our apartment where Lori was born before we moved to Kansas City for my orthopedic training. At 4:00 p.m. we stopped in front of our first house in Tulsa. When the limo pulled to a stop, so did the conversation as we all stared at the family landmark.

To the eight members of the family without a connection to the house, it probably looked like any house in an average neighborhood. I saw a home where we had planted prickly holly bushes set in white gravel beneath the kitchen window. Mary always wanted her kitchen window to face the front yard in order to watch over the safety and welfare of our girls. A concrete pad, one step up and no larger than a king-sized bed, defined the front porch. My original swing blew ever so slightly in the breeze, teasing my nostalgic self to take a couple of swings. Everyone remained seated in the limo as though a solemn preamble needed to be stated. Mary spoke up when she realized we were waiting on her.

"All day yesterday I thought about returning here to our old home. At first I was reluctant, but the more I mulled over the idea, the better it sounded." She leaned closer to the side window and strained to see up and down the street. "We haven't been by here in years."

Everyone leaned forward as if a family secret was about to be revealed. I picked up the story. "Two weeks before I completed orthopedic training in Kansas City, Mary, Lori, and Beth went ahead to Tulsa and stayed with your uncle Dick while Nana looked for a house. We returned to the Tulsa area because this was where our families were, where we grew up."

"Your Papa's only requirement for our new home," Mary said, "was that it be no more than ten minutes from work. He didn't care whether our home was a tree house, houseboat, or apartment."

"Some days in Kansas City I spent hours in our Volkswagen driving between hospitals, and just as I arrived home, I was called back. Cell phones had not been invented." Six grandkids raised their eyebrows and frowned at each other.

"And this is the house I found for us," Mary said. "We lived here seven years, until Lori was ten and Amy was three."

"So, come on," I said, waving my hand, "everybody out."

Family members milled about the sidewalk, not really knowing what to do while Nana stood in silence next to the curb. Unwilling to crowd her space, I stood behind her while she appeared to arrange the wholeness of her memories. She crinkled her eyes. Is this going to be a bust? Should I have given Mary more lead time? I didn't ask her if she was interested, I just told her we were going. She slowly walked up to the porch.

Todd answered the door with a pleasant smile and introduced himself to the family. "I learned more about you folks from neighbors after we talked. Welcome to your home. I'm headed next door. Please, take your time."

For our fiftieth anniversary, Mary and I could have toured the house by ourselves, but I wanted to bring our family to our Tulsa roots and tell stories about Lori, Beth, and Amy as children. Our grandkids needed to understand where their mothers and aunts had lived and played. *P U T   R Y A N*

We lined up on either side of the open door indicating Mary was to enter first. She picked up the cue and, after a moment's hesitation, stepped into the stranger's home. She faltered a few steps into the entryway. I did, too, momentarily overcome with a memory of walking into the house to tell Lori that Beth had died. I blindly followed Mary into the kitchen. Tears sprinkled down her cheeks as she surveyed the room. Through my own moist eyes, I recognized a long-forgotten stance: Mary leaning against the counter looking out the window into the front yard, monitoring the well-being of our girls.

Taking a deep breath, I eased into a kitchen chair with a view of the hall, waiting to hear Lori, Beth, and Amy squealing and running to me. Oblivious to the present, I reached for my young girls. No one saw me because our family had wandered ahead. When I thought of all of us together in the house, pleasing memories displaced ghosts of the past.

Sniffing the air, Mary turned and stepped to the sink. With a trembling hand she slid her fingers along the edges. "Beth had her first birthday cake in a highchair, right here next to the sink." She dragged her hand back and forth along the edge of the sink as though each stroke conjured another memory. Growing up in a house with a sink that had multiple chips and rust stains, her first evaluation of a kitchen, any kitchen, was to feel the sink. She opened cabinet doors and stared at dishes, perhaps seeing ours in their place. Closing one door and moving to the next, Mary stared into each cabinet while taking care not to touch personal property. She gave easy nods of approval as though memories spilled from behind each opened door. I watched and waited, afraid to blink and miss reading her emotional responses. More than anything, I wanted Mary to be pleased. Back in the hallway, she opened the entry closet, flicked on the light switch, and stared at the inside door trim. "Harold, look inside here."

Pencil marks revealed our girls' initials, heights, and dates that spanned their growth over seven years. Mary had made three neat columns, one for each girl: Lori, Beth, and Amy. Although the marks were two-dimensional, I couldn't resist running my fingers over them. My pulse quickened.

We stepped into the utility room and Mary ran her hand around the inside of another sink. "I bathed Beth in a little blue plastic tub in this sink, right here. I remember now how the edges of this sink felt. It hasn't changed." I nodded and listened, understanding Mary's mind resided in a far-off place. Then the furrow in her brow softened.

She was processing happy memories. "Thank you, Harold." Her mouth relaxed into a smile. Startled by the sudden change, I realized my anniversary plan was a success. Relief flooded through me. We wandered down to the master bedroom.

༜

Lori called from her old room down the hall. "Daddy, step in here." Everyone joined me. "This is the room where you gave me the empty refrigerator box, turned it on its side, and cut out two windows and two doors. I could run inside." She weaved her right hand back and forth like a minnow swimming upstream. "And I remember I liked it because adults were too big to get in. You chased me, slapping on the side of the box and grabbing at me through the windows and doors." She walked around the imaginary box. "You talked tough and grunted, and I squealed."

"This is it, kids," Amy said. "This is the room where Papa spawned the first box house. You just thought your big one was original."

Lori turned to me. "You just couldn't leave the idea alone until you'd built a monster that took a year and a half." Mary and my sons-in-law grinned and shook their heads.

While Lori and Amy guided their husbands and children through the house, recounting stories of their childhood, I lingered alone in the room with the imaginary box, hearing little girls' feet running, voices squealing. A surge of joy filled me. We all wandered together into the living room.

"This room always seemed so big back then," Lori said, pointing to an easy chair. "I fell off the sofa that sat there and cut my head. I bled all over Beth's blanket. Daddy, you held me on your lap and pressed a Kleenex to stop the bleeding. We watched cartoons together. I remember it was a Donald Duck cartoon. That was where you read *Where the Red Fern Grows* to us."

Mary and I stood in front of the fireplace. Now was my moment with everyone present.

"Here's where we lived and one of us died. We have let go of the bad, climbed out of more than one dark hole together, and embraced our good memories. This home is part of your story. Today we are braiding three generations. Thank you for coming, listening, and bringing your families. Your mother and I have weathered much in fifty years, just as you will. On a lighter note, me and this fireplace here about caused a divorce." Mary laughed and slipped a forgiving arm around my waist.

I explained how neither of us had ever enjoyed a fireplace at home while growing up. Most of the fireplaces we did see functioned as sources of heat for warmth and cooking. When I was a kid, a fire meant a place to burn trash in our backyard. Once or twice a year, we raked up remaining rusted cans and glass to haul to the city dump.

"Harold couldn't understand not to throw paper or food containers in our fireplace," Mary said.

"I couldn't help it. It was a source of entertainment to poke and explore. I learned how to pitch in ice cream cartons and food wrappers, then break up burned evidence with the poker."

"Harold, you were old enough to tell the difference between paper and wood ashes."

Was I?

"You rotated decorations on the mantle depending on the season: hearts, leprechauns, Easter eggs, flowers, pumpkins. You and the girls hung up four large Christmas stockings for us, plus a small one for Molly, our Heinz 57 family dog.

"We always placed the Christmas tree right here. Remember?" Mary said, pointing to the wall near the patio door.

"Do I ever!" I said. "As Kirk Douglas once sang..." Every hand around the room flew into the air with five fingers splayed. "I promise most of you have never heard the story I'm about to tell."

I explained how one Christmas season an article written by a local home-maintenance guru appeared in the newspaper about how to turn a dangerous flammable tree into a fireproof tree. His instructions said to take the tree outside and apply a special fireproofing preparation: two gallons water, one box baking soda, one cup Tide, one half cup salt, one cup Boraxo, and a few other household ingredients.

Mix well and sprinkle or slosh over all the limbs, starting at the top. Allow the solution time to dry and apply two more coats. Once dry, the final coating provided a fireproof shield that could not be seen. Our family bunched the limbs and dragged the tree back into the house to decorate it. Without sparing a single detail, I had puffed up my chest and told everyone who would listen about my actions as a responsible father. A friend even referred to me as Safety-Dad.

Eyeing the kids, I continued to explain that we kept the tree up for three weeks, until New Year's Day when we removed and stored the decorations.

"When Nana and your mothers left to run errands, I hauled the dry, undecorated, needle-shedding tree out stump first through the patio door to the backyard. Unbeknownst to Nana, I planned to test my fireproof tree, wanting confirmation of how safe the process had been. In case the tree burned for an extended time, it lay in the dry Bermuda grass well away from the house and wooden fence. I struck a match low under the thickest part of the tree.

"The tree did not burn, it exploded! Flames scorched my eyebrows and hair outlining my face, as well as hairs in my nose. I also set the yard on fire until it burned itself out at the cement patio."

I had staggered around the yard coughing smoke out of my lungs and stamping out the fire next to the fence using creative footwork. In a mirror inside I assessed my body and situation and, to my surprise, found no pain and nothing more serious than multiple small burn holes in my shirt that brought to mind Yosemite Sam after he lit Bugs's gunpowder room: scorched hair, face smudged with smoke, burnt pine needles.

"Too late to shower away the stink of a scorched backyard."

The grandkids' eyes grew large. "Is it still scorched?"

"Let's go see for ourselves," Mary said, as we exited through the sliding patio door.

"Nope," Sam announced.

I stood proudly by the trunk of a large pin oak with my hands in my armpits and rocked on my heels. "Mary, you dug the hole and planted this tree." Across the yard grew two evergreens. "And that one and that one. I was too busy to help; you were one tough lady."

Mary acknowledged me with a sweeping motion to the back fence. "That was a perfect place to hide Easter eggs," she said, "under those trees along the fence. Remember? The holly bushes had stickers, but that didn't stop the girls, just slowed 'em down."

Lori stood in the corner of the fence with both arms wide. "This is where we had the giant sand pile."

"Yeah," Mary said. "I called a local sand company and they told me a load of sand cost one dollar and delivery ten. I said I would take it but didn't know a load of sand contained nine cubic yards. The driver dumped the entire load in the corner and it piled up higher than the top of the fence." Mary threw her arm straight up and, bending her wrist, demonstrated the height of the pile. "In fact, some spilled over the fence into the neighbor's yard. Their kids loved it." She slapped her leg. "And after years of kids playing on the pile, it was still waist high. I'm surprised the fence didn't fall over."

As Lori stood next to Amy further explaining the giant sand pile, I studied my girls, realizing both of them had the same five-foot-two profile of Mary. All three could use the same shadow, except for the length of their carpet-thick brown hair:

"I *do* remember that sand pile," Amy said with glee. "I do! I do! I remember standing on top of the sand and seeing into the next yard."

Mary walked up next to me. "What are you looking at?"

"It's what I don't see: the old metal storage shed. Remember the night Lori and I ran for it in the rain? I knew hearing rain under the tin roof would be more dramatic than in the attic." Having watched my two older sisters tremble from rain, wind, and thunder, I wanted to teach Lori at an early age not to be afraid. That night I pulled down the folding ladder to the space above the garage. She followed me up to sit on boxes listening to rain pinging the roof. Shortly I came up with a better plan.

Mary's brows furrowed, her eyes blazed. "When I realized you two had run to the shed, I hollered to you about the storm warning on TV."

"And I hollered back that Lori would never forget hearing the rain and would learn to not be afraid of weather. As I expected, rain pounded the metal roof inches above our heads, thunder crashed, and the walls of our six-by-six-foot shed shook. Lots of drama. From the shed's door I could see your mouth moving while you waved us in. When the mother of all thunder claps broke directly over us, I slumped backwards. Lori witnessed my sudden fear."

"I thought it was fun until Daddy was scared," Lori said, "but I wasn't."

Mary frowned. "The two of you weren't three steps out of the shed before a burst of swirling wind picked it up and hurled it over our fence."

"Carrying it over two more fences and slamming it down on a picnic table two neighbors away," I said. "Just think what could have happened had we not … "

"So that's why you took our kids up to your attic one stormy night and read *Harry Potter*," Amy said.

"Yes. You caught me. You put the pieces together."

Along the east side of the house, I pointed to two evergreen trees I had planted six feet apart with a convenient water faucet between them. "Hey, kids," I said, working my way between overlapping limbs, spreading them wide, "I know where a secret water faucet is hidden." I opened the faucet behind a bush to prove my point. "Shazam!" Grandkids responded with the customary rolling of eyes, something they inherited from Mary.

In front of the house again, Amy pointed up and down the sidewalk. "Right here on this sidewalk is where I learned to ride a neighbor kid's bicycle. I remember now. Daddy, you gave me a push. And there's that mailbox I always ran into because I didn't know how to stop."

The rest of the family climbed into the limousine to wait patiently until we would leave for dinner. As if taking a second curtain call, Mary and I walked back inside our home, strolling at our own pace, hand in hand, relishing old memories like sitting at the breakfast table, sipping coffee, and deciding what to do with the kids on my next day off. We had lived here. Yes, we had lived here. Mary stood in the living room, eyes closed. "Shhh. Don't move or say anything," she said. "I'm watching the kids play under the Christmas tree."

My eyes filled with tears. When I planned this pilgrimage, I wondered how Mary might react, but never stopped to consider myself. Surprised by my own heightened emotions, by experiencing more than what I saw with my eyes, I also felt it in my gut. Our journey back became a validation that our memories together were real. Life happened here because of us.

After a prolonged silence, Mary and I looked at each other. I raised my eyebrows and shrugged my shoulders.

"I'm ready," she said.

I pulled a prewritten thank-you card from my pocket and left it on the kitchen counter. On the way out, we stopped in the entry hall and turned to look into the living room one last time. "It's okay to visit the past, isn't it?" I said, looking into her glistening eyes.

"As long as we don't live there," Mary said.

"Hope so, 'cause I've been doing a lot of it lately. When I knew we were going to visit our old home, I found it difficult to keep the past out of the present," I said.

Together we gazed unfocused at the places where activities once took place, where our lives played out for seven years. Mary reached for my hand. I moved behind her with my hands cupped around her waist and hands and said, "It's been a good ride."

"We've taken our licks, but we're like crabgrass. You can't kill us. We just keep coming back," she said.

Walking out the door together, Mary released her hand from mine. She ran fingers over the closed door as though she could read all of our past, in that house, through the door, memories of a different time.

I wasn't sad to close the door; home is wherever Mary is. Still on the porch, I said, "Mary, come swing with me." We gently swayed back and forth.

"Thank you," she said, holding my face in her hands. "Let's do another fifty years," and then she planted a kiss on me.

"If the next fifty years are half as fun as the last fifty, it will be a hoot!" I said.

"Nothing involving fire, okay?"

"Deal. Besides, we'll have a crop of great-grandkids coming along someday for us to play with, and I have at least another dozen ideas I want to try out on 'em."

"Let's do it, then," Mary said, taking my hand, "let's go home."

Harold and Mary, 50 Years in Love

About the Author

An orthopedic surgeon, Dr. Harold Battenfield established the Department of Orthopedics at Tulsa Regional Medical Center in 1975, and served as department chair for seventeen years. Responsible for starting the post-graduate training programs in orthopedic surgery at the center, he was its director for twenty-one years and primary trainer for 34 orthopedic residents. He holds three medical-device patents.

Dedicated to his family, experiential learning adventures around the world, and the osteopathic profession, he lives in Tulsa with his wife, Mary.

Oscar and Eller
Battenfield

Devoe and Julia
Battenfield

Harold and Mary
Battenfield

Lori, Mary, Amy

Stewart Family:
Doug, Sam, Jack, Lori, Max

King Family:
Keegan, Amy, Kevin, Lauren, Grant

Acknowledgments

Thank you to Mary Battenfield, my wife, for giving me love and space enough to write, and all five generations of my family, for they are the stories; Stephanie Colburn, my chief editor, who kept me on track, listened well, and inspired me with her tough questions; Dennis Letts, for encouraging me to write a book based on stories of my grandkids; Billie Letts, for providing objective support for my early chapters; Jack Stewart, for the help with computer technology; Writers Group members, for offering their enthusiastic encouragement for five years: John Carletti, Cathy Newsome, Ken Tracy, Nancy Whitman, and Stephanie Colburn; and to Sarah Stecher, for teaching thirty-six hours of formal classes that became the backbone of my writing education after retirement.

"Does that sign say 50 mph?"